FROM SHARECROPPER TO MULTIMILLIONAIRE

A BIOGRAPHY OF LORENZO PITTS

S. CLAUDIA LANG PITTS

with
DR. LORENZO PITTS, JR.

Lorenzo Pitts, Sr. An American Story

Copyright © 2025 by S Claudia Lang-Pitts

All rights reserved.

No part of this book may be reproduced in any form or by any electronic or mechanical means, including information storage and retrieval systems, without written permission from the author, except for the use of brief quotations in a book review.

Cover Design: Raegahn Rebstock
Interior Design: Teresa Evans

Portrait of Lorenzo Pitts, Sr.
Artist: Charles Scogins

ISBN paperback 978-1-967213-00-9

Published 2025 by Publish Authority,
300 Colonial Center Parkway, Suite 100
Roswell, GA, USA
PublishAuthority.com

Printed in the United States of America

CONTENTS

Foreword	xi
Prologue	1
CHAPTER 1 *Father and Son*	5
Reconstruction and Sharecropping	8
Memories of Early Life	9
CHAPTER 2 *World War II*	15
A Love Story – Memories of Helen	21
CHAPTER 3 *Helen: "The Promise"*	30
CHAPTER 4 *Early Memories of Sons*	33
El Dorado	36
CHAPTER 5 *World War II Navy Buddy*	40
CHAPTER 6 *A New Beginning*	44
Return to Roxbury	49
Lorenzo Sr. Shares His Feelings	52
Memories of the San Diego Family	56
Lorenzo Sr. Speaks to Lorenzo Jr.	59
Our Plans vs God's Plans	66
The Next Generation	67
CHAPTER 7 *Lorenzo Pitts, Jr.'s Life History*	76
Death of Reverend Claude Lang	83
Death of Lorenzo Pitts	85
Family Turmoil	87

CHAPTER 8 *Managing the Estate*	90
U.S. Department of Housing and Urban Development (HUD)	93
CHAPTER 9 *How to Steal Intergenerational Wealth*	95
The Story Behind the Story	97
Summary of Estate Plan and Will	110
CHAPTER 10 *My Dad - Patriarch Lorenzo Pitts, Sr.*	112
Epilogue	118
THE ESTATE OF LORENZO PITTS, SR.	121
Acknowledgments	123
Appendices	129
APPENDIX A *Curriculum Vitae S Claudia Lang Pitts*	131
APPENDIX B *Suffolk, SS. Probate and Family Court In RE: Estate of Lorenzo Pitts*	133
APPENDIX C *TERRY K. MOND and WILLETTA PITTS-GIVENS*	136
I. INTRODUCTION	136
II. PROCEDURAL HISTORY	137
APPENDIX D *Appellate Court of Massachusetts*	138
APPENDIX E *Sequence of Legal Events*	139
APPENDIX F *Historical and Family Timeline*	141
APPENDIX G *Tributes and Awards*	146
Awards – Plaques (Subcollection)	147
APPENDIX H *Mond/Pitts Correspondence*	154
APPENDIX I *Media Articles*	160

APPENDIX J   165
Suggested Reading List and Videos

APPENDIX K   168
Photo Archives

Notes   185

This book is dedicated to the memory of

Frank Walton Eastland, CEO of Publish Authority,

who was a resolute and firsthand publisher, mentor, and friend. Frank was there for the encouragement, editing, and publishing of

"The Soul Of Our Family"

and

"From Sharecropper to Multimillionaire."

Thank you, Frank. R.I.P.

A job well done!

April 1947 – September 2025

But there is some satisfaction
That is mighty sweet to take,
When you've reached a destination
That you thought you couldn't make.

Author Anonymous

FOREWORD
BY NANCY JOHNSON-BISHOP

Intergenerational wealth transfer is not very common in the African American community. This is a wonderful true story of one Black man's fight to pass wealth down to the next generation. Many African American families have lost valuable real estate and wealth due to theft, delinquent taxes, urban renewal, and family dysfunction. Even a last Will and Testament is no guarantee of a safeguard for rightful heirs! The stories are innumerable.

In this brilliant and gripping book, there is a story, beautifully told by the those who lived it. A family who rose from the fields of generational sharecropping to the ranks of wealth known in this country to only a few families of African descent. Wealth, not attained by gambling or speculation, but wealth achieved by astute hard work and perseverance. It is the chronology of three generations of sharecroppers and the rise to the rank of real estate magnate in one of the least Black cities in America! This is the story of Lorenzo Pitts, Sr. of Boston, Massachusetts!

The struggles of this family may be familiar to many Black families – but not the outcome! Many have only to go back one generation for examples of black wealth stolen or squandered and lost forever. Too often, family members found that quick money was available by selling property and businesses to unscrupulous investors for a fraction of the true value of the property or for unpaid property taxes, shutting the door on the "American Dream" forever.

Lack of "last will and testaments" often provided an opportunity for family battles. It was not a guarantee! Distrust in the judicial system led, and continues to lead many black families to avoid the filing of legal final documents. Even so, a last will and testament does not always protect legal beneficiaries from the loss of their inheritance. Without proper legal representation, we find that courts very seldom give serious consideration to proper dispensation of inheritances. Many families end up in intense court battles lasting decades or more despite having legal wills and proof of ownership. Too often, the biggest beneficiary of the decedent's assets is the lawyer!

This is the story of a black family that migrated from Texas during the Great Migration to New England after World War II. They made a life for themselves in Boston during the Jim Crow Laws period and through the Civil Rights Movement. They overcame the poverty that entrapped families, neighbors, and friends. Industrialization had already impacted farming and sharecropping as they knew it. But It would ultimately take a family from the bitter taste of third-generation sharecropping to the pinnacle of American wealth! This is the true story of a family that dared to take on the establishment that had the intent of robbing them of their legacy, and the right to claim what was rightfully theirs. This is the story of grit, faith, and love that only culminates in the twenty-first century! It is an inspirational story of endurance, sacrifice and tenacity for readers who may face or may be facing similar challenges. .... The story of Lorenzo Pitts, Sr., and Mond vs. Pitts.

Nancy Johnson-Bishop
Educator, Classical Pianist

NOTE:
All scripture references are from the King James Version of the Bible. Any errors or omissions in this book are unintentional.

Foreword

Lorenzo Pitts, Sr. An American Story

PROLOGUE

"This is the story of my father, who had an extraordinarily complex life. He was a very intelligent and successful entrepreneur and businessman who thrived despite the shackles of Jim Crow. He was a descendant of generations of sharecroppers. He experienced family tribulations in the untimely deaths of loved ones, the parenting of twelve children, borderline poverty, and institutional racism in Boston, Massachusetts."
— *Lorenzo Pitts, Jr.*

It was Saturday, July 10, 1948, an ordinarily warm afternoon in San Diego, California. The sky was blue and clear except for the cumulus clouds that seemed to float above like delicate white cotton. There was a refreshing summer breeze that cooled the air.

The San Diegan passenger train to Los Angeles had pulled into the railway station fifteen minutes prior. The platform that was once bustling with travelers loaded down with their luggage was now empty, except for Lorenzo, Sr. He stood near the end of the platform, facing the baggage car with his suitcase and baby Robert in his arms. Lorenzo, Jr., also known as Sonny by his parents, was standing at his side, struggling to hold on to a bag that contained a lunch box with food that his grandmother, Minnie, had given him, diapers, and other items for the baby.

Lorenzo, Sr., watched as four baggage handlers loaded the wooden box containing Helen's casket. Time seemed to stand still. A porter broke the silence by beckoning Lorenzo to come to the train car designated for Black passengers. This would be the start of a long memorable journey to El Dorado, Arkansas. During this period of travel, the Jim Crow 'Separate Coach Law of 1891' was in full force. The law required separate coaches on railway trains for White and Black passengers.

The U.S. Supreme Court's 'Separate but equal' clause in the *"Plessy v. Ferguson"* ruling upheld state-imposed Jim Crow laws until 1955, when the Federal Interstate Commerce Commission decreed that all racial segregation on interstate passenger trains and buses must end by January 10, 1956. In Arkansas, Helen's home state, the law was finally repealed in 1973.

Lorenzo boarded the Rock Island train (known as The Golden State) with Helen and their two sons. He and his boys started the long journey to her hometown, El Dorado, Arkansas. The journey required changing trains several times, loading and unloading. From the San Diegan train to Los Angeles, changing to The Rock Island train to Chicago, Illinois, and finally transferring to the Pacific Railroad bound for El Dorado, Arkansas. Whenever they transferred from one train to the next, he would always watch the baggage handlers carrying the wooden box that contained Helen's casket. His heart was heavy. His spirit was fragile. He would not rest until Helen was home in El Dorado, Arkansas.

Soon after boarding the train to Chicago, Lorenzo was approached by several Colored women who asked, "Are you traveling with those babies by yourself?"

He said, "Yes, and no. I'm not alone."

They replied, "Well, what happened?"

"These are my two boys. Their mother is in the baggage car in a casket on this train. We're headed to El Dorado, Arkansas, where her funeral and burial will be."

Upon hearing about his troubles, the ladies offered to help

Lorenzo care for three-and-a-half-month-old Robert and toddler Lorenzo, Jr. while enroute. They did everything for the boys – everything, and Lorenzo felt that he finally had a chance to relax a little, if you could call it relaxing. His worries were filled with what he had promised Helen before she passed and what he had to do to fulfill those promises. Deep down, he knew that he had to keep his promise to his first love, his precious wife. He had sworn to Helen. With her last breath in response, she said, "I'm satisfied."

The train ride was comforting to grief-stricken Lorenzo. The previous days had been filled with excruciating emotional pain and confusion resulting from Helen's illness and death at age 23. He had already become a widower at age 24, a father of two small children with an undetermined future. But one thing Lorenzo was sure of was that there would be no sharecropping in his future.

Plessy v. Ferguson produced a wave of segregation laws and ordinances that affected the lives of Blacks and whites (Image courtesy Birmingham Public Library).

The Separate Coach Law of 1891 (Act 17) was a Jim Crow law requiring separate coaches on railway trains for white and black passengers. The law arose out of the political upheavals of the era, in which the Democratic Party sought to stave off challenges to their dominance by distracting voters with racist concerns, and it further relegated African Americans to the margins of social and economic life.[1] Encyclopedia of Arkansas.

> *"We see a hearse; we think sorrow. We see a grave; we think despair. We hear of a death; we think of a loss. Not so in heaven. When heaven sees a breathless body, it sees the vacated cocoon & the liberated butterfly."* [2]
> — *Max Lucado, Christian author and preacher.*

1

FATHER AND SON

TAPED RECOLLECTION OF LORENZO PITTS, JR.'S TELEPHONE CONVERSATION WITH LORENZO PITTS, SR.

One December evening in 2005, I was sitting at the desk in my home office in Atlanta, Georgia, relaxing and feeling great elation, having just received a confirmation letter that my PhD Dissertation had been accepted by Clark Atlanta University's Dissertation Committee. My phone rang. It was my father who lived in Boston. Dad was an infrequent caller. His call made my ears perk up. I said, "Hi, how are you?"

He said, "Okay." in a low voice.

He proceeded to tell me that several of his business contemporaries, including his business partner, had recently passed away.

He asked, "What do you think would happen if I passed away tomorrow?"

I replied, "The IRS (Internal Revenue Service) would be your partner." Silence followed.

He said, "I don't think I like that." More silence.

Then he said, "Is there anything we can do about it?

I said, "Yes." I continued, "The first thing we must do is to retain an estate/probate attorney."

He said he would check with his business attorney and his accountant for leads and referrals.

In January 2006, Dad and I had a three-way conference call with Attorney Terry Mond from a law firm in Quincy, Massachusetts. Attorney Mond had been retained to develop the estate plan: Part 1 – Living, Part 2 – After Death. Dad wanted to retain maximum control during his lifetime. Working with Attorney Mond, we continued to discuss and develop the estate plan. It was completed, signed, notarized, and registered with the Suffolk County Probate Court in July 2007.

In May of 2006, Dad attended my graduation at Clark Atlanta University in Atlanta. Dr. Charles R. Stith, Director of Boston University's African Presidential Center and former United States Ambassador to Tanzania, was the Commencement speaker. In December of 2006, Dr. Stith was the guest speaker at our family's Annual Christmas Holiday Banquet in Boston and spoke to the family about the importance and role of the Black family in business and community. It was an opportunity for all of Dad's children to fellowship together.

During Dad's visit to Atlanta for my graduation, we had a chance to discuss the ongoing development of the Estate Plan and other family and business matters. It was during this visit that I asked Dad if he would tell me about my mother, who died when I was 2 years old, and my brother Robert was three-and-a-half months old. I also told him I would like to know about his life in Texas, his family, and how he met my mother.

My wife Claudia purchased a tape recorder and a couple boxes of tapes for Dad to take back to Boston with him. It was our desire to capture Dad's memories and stories of his life not just for myself but for Robert and current and future generations.

In the Spring of 2007, I received a box in the mail from Dad containing several recording tapes. Claudia and I were ecstatic and anxious to hear what the tapes revealed. Dad had done what I requested. Putting everything on hold sitting in the quiet of my office, we took out all the tapes and organized them in listening order. It was time to be silent and listen to the audio tapes.

Though you have made me see troubles, many and bitter, you will restore my life again; from the depths of the earth, you will again bring me up. You will increase my honor and comfort me once again.
Psalm 71:20-21

Reconstruction and Sharecropping

In the early years of Reconstruction, it was general knowledge that most Colored people living in rural areas of the South were left without land and forced to work as laborers on large white-owned farms and plantations in order to earn a living and survive. There were many clashes with former owners bent on re-establishing a gang-labor system similar to the one that prevailed under slavery.

Sharecropping after the Civil War was just a small step from enslavement. Sharecroppers, though free, were enslaved to a landowner by debt. The sharecropper did all of the work, took all of the risks, and got extraordinarily little in return.

In an effort to regulate the labor force and reassert white supremacy in the South, legislative officials in former Confederate states soon passed restrictive laws denying Colored people legal equality or political rights and created Black codes that forced the formerly enslaved to sign yearly labor contracts or be arrested and jailed for vagrancy.

In January 1865, in an effort to address the issues caused by the growing number of refugees, General Sherman issued Special Field Order Number 15 as a temporary plan granting each freed family 40 acres of land on the islands and coastal region of Georgia. The Union Army also donated some of its mules to the formerly enslaved people. In 1870, around 30,000 African Americans in the South owned land (small plots), compared to the 4 million others who did not.

When the War ended with the surrender of General Robert E. Lee, many freed Black people saw the "40 acres and a mule" policy as proof that they would finally be able to work their own land after years of servitude. Owning land was the key to economic independence and autonomy. However, in April of 1865, President Abraham Lincoln was assassinated. Immediately thereafter, Vice President Johnson assumed the presidency, and pardoned all of the former Confederate secessionists, and returned all their property.

Memories of Early Life

Taped Recollection of Lorenzo Pitts, Sr.

My Great-grandfather, Napoleon Pitts, was born and enslaved in Mississippi in 1846. My Grandfather, Albert Pitts (Bd. 1870), and my father Napoleon Pitts (Bd.1899) were both sharecroppers. For generations, my family tilled the land and harvested crops in Texas, migrating from Gonzales to Hillsboro, Sherman, Waco, and Lockhart.

My family lived for several years in Sherman, a small town located in northeast Texas in Grayson County. It was a modest southern town with a lot of racial turmoil, and a lot of horrific things transpired, including lynching.

From the General Negative Collection, North Carolina State Archives, call #: N_83_7_30, Raleigh, NC.

When I was a young boy, an angry White mob lynched a 41-year-old Black man named George Hughes, who died on May 9th, 1930. He was lynched inside the town center square. At that time, I tried to understand why and how something so cruel and gruesome could happen. In later years, hearsay revealed that the Black man, George Hughes, was working for a local white farmer, and, for some reason, a White woman entered the house while he was working and accused him of rape.

The White woman said, "This nigger raped me, this nigger raped me!"

Shortly after, many people started running after him, and he headed into town to the courthouse for help and protection. We lived near the center of town. My father said he remembered seeing groups of people running toward the center of town. He said that Mr. Hughes ran into the courthouse for safety. Once inside, he ran up the stairs and hid in a small room at the top of the courthouse. They couldn't find him, but they knew that he was hiding in the building, so they asked all of the White people that had guns and rope to assist with his capture.

I ask my father, "Why are they doing that?"

My father answered, "I don't understand it either, why do they want to kill him? They're saying that he raped someone. But as he was running toward the courthouse, he was crying out, 'I did not rape her, I did not rape her! She is lying! I did not do that!' They made everyone leave the building. After the building was cleared, they sprinkled gasoline throughout the building and set it on fire."[1] [2]

From Sharecropper to Multimillionaire

George Huges in custody of law enforcement shortly before his ungodly and dastardly lynching

The corpse of George Hughe's body after being hanged, burned, and mutilated. According to eyewitness accounts, there were several pictures taken of his corpse, many of which were snapped by enthusiastic locals

My father said that he watched the building burn. He remembered the hot air and the enormous blaze of fire. The building burned all day. After the blaze subsided, the bricks were surprisingly still standing. [3]

From Sharecropper to Multimillionaire

Sherman Courthouse Burning. The Burning of the Grayson county courthouse

The angry mob thought they could still find George Hughes despite his attempts to hide. So, they used the ladder from the fire engine to access the top of the building. They found George Hughes in the small machine room at the top of the building.

Later, the Colored section of town was burned down. Many Colored people in the town started fleeing.

Shortly after the lynching and the burning of the town, my grandfather, Napoleon, became ill and remained ill for quite some time. So, my father decided it was time to move to Lockhart, Texas, where my grandparents lived, to help his father. He felt they could work on the farm together as a family.

It was a large farm consisting of more than 300 acres. My parents and my five brothers and sisters plowed the land, planted, cultivated, and harvested crops like cantaloupe, corn, beans, carrots, potatoes, peas, and numerous other crops. The only food products that our family needed to purchase were sugar, salt, and flour. Father would take our corn to the mill to have it finely minced to use for cornbread, grits, and other food products. At the end of the growing season, the family would load the wagon and take the crops into town to sell. Several years after we arrived on the farm, my grandfather died after a lifetime of hard work and struggle.

It was a never-ending cycle marked by extremely demanding work and much uncertainty, and left me feeling hopeless for a better future than my grandfather and father ever knew.

2

WORLD WAR II

This is the second tape. I am now attempting to record what you are most, perhaps, interested in. I'm going to skip over most of my youth and teenage years, growing up, going to school, working hard, and doing different things. During that time, I thought it was a lot of fun. We did a lot of things and were very pleased with the things that we had a chance to do.

I'm going to skip over that time and turn the clock forward. I'm going to start at the time when World War II broke out: when the world went to War. I realized at that time that I had an opportunity to do something for my father and mother so that they could be able to help themselves and go beyond sharecropping and enjoy a different life than what they were forced to live and did live most of their lives.

I joined the military (Navy). I was not drafted. I volunteered. I volunteered to serve. But before that, let me back up a little bit. To talk about the time before I went into the service, I asked my father if he would sign an affidavit and state that I was older than I really was. He asked me why. I told him I wanted to join the service. I explained to him what I was going to do. I explained to him that I was going to make out an allotment. I was aware that I would receive some money. He said, "Let me think about this awhile."

Two or three days went by, and one day, he said, "I have thought about this. I cannot; I just cannot sign an affidavit for you to go to War to fight. You might get killed, and I will never forgive myself."

I said, "I don't feel that I will get killed. I think I will survive. I want to go. I can make it."

Now, I recall what he was telling me. "You've never been away from home. You'll be going a long distance. Then you'll be going overseas, and no telling what will happen."

I recall having this wonderful discussion, and I told him, "I am ready to go; I have made up my mind. I want to help you, and this is one way I feel that I can."

Then he said, "I am very deeply saddened, and I regret that I cannot sign the affidavit for you. I cannot have this on my conscience. If I do, I will never forgive myself."

I recall looking at him. We were standing close together. And he looked away as if he was looking over the high-rises into the mountains. In my mind, I felt that he was asking God to forgive him if he did not sign. And I felt that he was real. And I knew that if he said he would not sign, then he would not sign.

I recall it as if it was just yesterday. I said, "I wanted you to know I came to you first. If you do not sign, I know mother will sign, but I want you to know."

And he said to me, "I'm sorry, I cannot sign."

I said, "OK, so you don't have to worry about it. Whatever would be on your conscience will no longer be there because you did not sign it. But I know Mother will sign it."

"So, I went and asked her, would she sign. The reason I needed her to sign, because at that time I was 16, and you had to be 17 years old. I wanted her to sign on the affidavit that I was 17. I went to her, and I explained to her what I wanted to do and the reason I wanted to do it. And how badly I wanted to do it, and there was nothing that I would ever accept more than just going into the service so I could be some help to her and Dad. I felt I could help."

During World War II, more than 2.5 million African American men registered for the draft, and African American women volunteered in large numbers. When combined with Black women enlisted in the Women's Army Corps, more than one million African Americans served in the Army during the War. The Army, Navy, and Marine Corps all segregated African Americans into separate units because of the belief that they were not as capable as white service members. For more than 200 years, African Americans have served courageously in every conflict in U.S. history. They endured individual and institutional racism while fighting for social equality and opportunity.

Yes, Mama signed it. Then, I went down to the military recruiting office. They questioned me and accepted the affidavit.

> Date of entry into active service: 2/17/1942, Austin, Texas
> Date of Separation: 10/17/45, Final Rating: Steward Second Class
> Character of Separation: Honorable
> American Theatre, European Theatre (1) Star, Presidential Unit Citation (1), Good Conduct[1]

Photo: New recruits receive their first lecture on Naval Procedure. Chief Specialist in khaki demonstrated the proper way to wear a navy hat (9-9-42, National Archives

So, it was! I volunteered and went into the service. From there, I went from Austin to Houston by bus. We had a whole busload of men. In Houston, we got on the train. We took the train from Houston to Norfolk, Virginia. Norfolk is where I took my training. At the time we called it, you took your boot training. Boot training means you were a recruit in the service.

We did all the things that one needs to do. I did all the tests. I passed them all. And then, after I had graduated, after the recruiting stage of the service, I went on the ship.

https://en.wikipedia.org.wiki.USSNitro:(AE-2)

From Sharecropper to Multimillionaire

The Class AE-2 was an ammunition carrier; it was called Nitro.[2] The USS Nitro was loaded down with all kinds of heavy explosives, and it would get into what we call a convoy. It would be in the middle of a convoy, and it would sail across the ocean, the Atlantic. And then we unloaded the ship. The ammunition was for the soldiers. I was on the ship, I believe, for about a year; I'm not too sure. And then I went back to Norfolk, Virginia. I received orders that I was going to be transferred. I was going to be transferred from the Nitro to a new ship just put into commission, a brand-new ship called Destroyer Escort, the name of it was the Francis M. Robinson DE 220, Destroyer Escort, that's what the DE means."

https://en.wikipedia.org/wiki/USS_Francis_M._Robinson[8]

Before I was transferred to the Destroyer Escort (DE) ship,[3] I could not stand the Navy uniform. I worked extremely hard, trying to do the work, everything that one needs to do to advance himself to a higher rank. I was the youngest chief petty officer in the service. I was very alert, I understood how to cook, and that was my job. I was a steward. My job was to put together the menu and prepare the food for the officers. That was my job. I was in charge of all the officers' food preparations. I put a menu together and prepared their food, three meals a day, different menus, different foods for each meal of the day. That was what I did, and that was my job.

A Love Story – Memories of Helen

This particular guy, his name was Buck Montgomery. Buck used to ask me would I please write a letter to someone for him.

I said, "Of course," and I did.

I always had good handwriting and penmanship. Buck's writing was so bad, I'm telling you, you couldn't tell an M from an N, a T or an I from an E. Oh, his handwriting was terrible. And he asked me if I would write to his girlfriend. I said, "Yes, I would do it."

I said, "What is your girlfriend's name?"

He said, "Her name is Helen."

I said, "Ok, yes, I will do it."

I wrote letters for him month after month. When Helen sent a letter, I'd read the letter to him and told him what she was saying in the letter. But in the letters, she never talked about him being her boyfriend. She never said, "I love you." She never said, "I'll be glad when you come home."

The closest thing that she ever said to him, that maybe she cared, was, "I hope you don't get hurt. I hope you don't get killed, and take care of yourself."

At the end of the letter, she would just sign, 'Helen.' She had nice handwriting.

During the time I was writing for him, I started writing a page for myself because she kept asking him, "Who is this person that's writing for you? Whoever the person is that is writing this letter for you, tell him hello. And then tell him I'm glad you've written to me, and that he's writing for you. That is a wonderful thing for him to do."

After about three months, I started writing a letter for myself to Helen and putting it inside Buck's letter.

When you're in the service, you have a lot of time; time on your hands. Time that you will never, never run out of. So, I used to sit and think about how I was going to write and what I was going to say.

I remember I used to write Helen and say, "I have never seen you. All I can say is I love the way you write, and I believe I love you." I used to write two or three lines and say, "Helen, I love you, I love you, I love you. I would like to see how you look." I asked her if she would please send me a picture of herself. I was sending letters to her often. Buck never knew that I was writing personal letters to Helen.

She stopped writing to him as often. Maybe once a month, he would get a letter. Whenever he received a letter, he would ask me to write a response. Then, I would write a letter for him. But by that time, I would have already written two or three letters to Helen from me.

She sent me a picture. I thought it was so cute, so beautiful. And I told Buck, I said, "Buck, Helen sent me a picture and in her letter" …Wait, I'm going ahead of myself.

I asked her many times in many letters I've written, "Is Buck your boyfriend? Are you Buck's girlfriend?"

She continued to say in the letter, "No, no, he's just somebody I know. He lived in the community where I live. I just know him as a friend. He is not my boyfriend. I am not his girlfriend. Please, believe me."

I said, "OK, if you're not his girlfriend, send me a picture of you, and I will show him a picture that you sent to me. And if you really care, tell me in your letter that you care for me and you believe you love me."

She wrote back in the letter and said, "Yes, Lorenzo, I love you. Here is my picture. Send me a picture of you."

I sent her a picture of me, and I showed Buck the picture of her, and he said, "Yes, that is Helen. Isn't she beautiful?"

I said, "Yes."

He said, "Let me keep the picture for a while."

I said, "No, this picture was sent to me. You lied to me. You told me that Helen was your girlfriend. She repeatedly has told me you are not her boyfriend. She is not your girlfriend. And I believed her."

And then he says, "Well, I claimed her because she was the prettiest girl in our community where we lived."

I said, "OK. If she is not your girlfriend, I am going to continue to write her."

And he said, "OK, but will you keep writing a letter for me?"

I said, "OK, I will write. I will answer her letters whenever she writes you."

She used to write and ask me, "Do you want me to stop writing Buck?"

At first, I told her, "It's ok, you can keep writing him."

She said, "I will answer his letters back and forth, and If you do not want me to write to him anymore, I promise you I will never write to him again."

And, when she stated that, after the many letters that had been written, I told her in my next letter that I would like to come and see her.

And she responded, "Yes, I would like it."

I called her on the telephone. We started talking back and forth and writing letters. I guess I must have written two or three letters a week because I had a lot of time on my hands, and I could do it. And when I got a furlough, furlough means when I got a leave, I believe I had two weeks at a time. Instead of me going home, I went to Arkansas…. El Dorado, Arkansas. That's where I went, to see Helen. Sonny, that is where I met your mother, Helen.

We spent time together. Every day we were together, and I was so pleased. During the time we were together on that furlough, I asked her if she would be my wife.

And she said, "Yes."

I said, "When I get back to Norfolk, and get back on the ship, I will buy an engagement ring and send it to you. Will you wear it? I remember it as if it was just yesterday or today.

She said, "I will wear it, and I will never pull it off."

I said, "Oh, I love it. You have made my life worthwhile." We talked about most of the things that two young individuals that fell in love with each other talk about. The next time I got a furlough, again, instead of going home, I went to Arkansas, and we got married on January 24, 1945. That was a pleasure. That was so wonderful. We got married, and now, I had to go back to the ship. I had to leave her.

That was the time when we had to make plans for how she was going to get to New York. That's where the ship was going to be, at New York City Harbor. She would be going to a big city where she had never been, and I, too, knew nothing about New York City.

A friend of mine who was on the ship with me, named Thomas Middleton, had a sister and brother who lived in New York City. They were from Charleston, South Carolina. I remember his sister's name, Bernita, just as if it was yesterday. I spoke on the phone with Bernita, and we discussed Helen's trip to New York City.

Bernita said, "Yes, I will meet her at the train station."

Bernita and Helen spoke on the phone and agreed to wear a special-colored dress so that they would be able to spot each other at the train station.

When the time came for Helen's arrival, I was not in New York City. My ship was on the high seas. When the ship returned to New York City Harbor, Middleton and I went immediately to his sister's house. And what can you guess? There was Helen.

We went through a long reunion, walking, laughing, and talking about how life would be. And how we met, and how Bernita and she recognized each other because of the color of the clothes they had on that day. That was the most joyful time that anyone could ever experience in life.

Life is so wonderful; life has such a great purpose.

My ship left New York City and went to Boston. By that time, the War was almost over. Helen was still living in New York City with Bernita. I paid Bernita for her to stay there, to live there. She would buy her own food and cook. I told her she would not be a burden on anyone.

About the time the ship arrived in Boston, I was getting ready to get discharged. However, I could not leave the ship. I could not be discharged until someone came on board that could relieve me of my duties because I was a chief petty officer in the commissary department, and someone had to come with a rank that could carry on the duties. I was on the ship there in Boston because the War was over. I believe it was approximately six months longer than I was supposed to stay.

At that time, I had gotten a place here in Boston when Helen arrived from New York. And that's where we started to spend time together as husband and wife because we were near each other. Oh, what a wonderful time. During the time we spent together, I was under the impression that she had an illness. Also, around the first of every month, she used to get sick. The doctors that she had been visiting in El Dorado told her that when she gets married that would no longer happen because the reason she got sick and felt faint is because her hormones were so rich, and she needed a husband.

I was so happy and pleased to know that I was the first and only one that Helen ever knew as a man.

Lorenzo took joy in knowing he would be Helen's first intimate relationship. Helen tried to explain to Lorenzo about her illness from her time as a young woman. Whenever she menstruated, she would get really faint and could hardly sit up or stand. The doctors in El Dorado all diagnosed similar illnesses, and they didn't think that there was anything that could be done on Helen's behalf. However, one of the doctors prescribed a medication that helped alleviate the side effects of the underlying issue for a brief time.

Lorenzo reflected on their courtship when he asked Helen to be his wife.

"What about my illness?" Helen said to him in response. "I have told you everything, the kind of suffering I go through. Do you still want me to be your wife?"

"Yes," Lorenzo responded. "You've been honest with me, and I understand and respect your honesty. I want to be your husband."

"Okay, as long as you know the truth. I have told you everything, my conscience is clear, and I'm not keeping anything from you," Helen replied.

He believed Helen to be a straightforward and honest person. He felt extremely blessed that he was able to meet a lady like her and have her as his wife.

Life in Boston was challenging for them, as it was for many of the Black Bostonians who had migrated from the South during the great migration, but their time together was incredibly happy. It wasn't long before Helen got pregnant. Her menstrual period stopped, but her fainting problem persisted during the pregnancy. She recognized the fainting symptoms before the fainting occurred. She would sit and relax for an hour or so or take a nap. After her rest, Helen would always be okay, or she seemed to be okay. Their first child, a son, was born at Boston City Hospital on May 19, 1946, and given the name of Lorenzo Pitts, Jr., a name they both proudly agreed on.

Sometime after the birth of their son, Helen began to have recurring bouts of illness. Lorenzo immediately placed Helen under the care of physicians at the Boston City Hospital. The so-called 'specialist' examined her numerous times and tried a wide range of diverse treatments. But, similar to the doctors in El Dorado, they repeatedly proclaimed they could not diagnose Helen's health problem. The doctors felt the medication prescribed to her should have corrected the problem, and it never did. The doctors told Lorenzo that they just did not know what was wrong. They did not know what the next steps would be to cure Helen of the ailment that was causing her distress. However, specialized healthcare and medical diagnoses for Black women during the 1940s were wanting in quantity and quality.

Lorenzo recalled several occasions when he had to take Helen to the emergency room after she experienced an episode of fainting. After an incident, she would sleep for three or four hours, and that worried him.

One day, while at work, he received a call from the Boston City Hospital, so he rushed to the hospital. When he arrived, Helen's doctor was standing near the nursing station. Recognizing him as Helen's husband, he explained to Lorenzo that his wife had died. As he was walking towards Helen's room, a nurse approached him and said,

"I'm very sorry, but there was nothing that we could have done to help your wife."

When he entered the room, Helen, surprisingly, was sitting up in bed. She was still alive! What a moment! Lorenzo put his arms around her and asked how she felt.

She said, "I'm feeling much better now. Are you going to take me home now?"

"Yes," Lorenzo said. He called the nurse, and the nurse stuck her head in the door.

"What do you want?" she asked.

"My wife wants to speak with you. I want to take her home."

"What?" the nurse cried out. She dashed inside the room, and when she saw Helen sitting up in bed, she fainted.

The nurse, along with the doctor and others, had mistakenly told Lorenzo that Helen had passed as soon as he arrived at the hospital corridor. But Helen, who was without family or friends during that time, held on to see her husband, Lorenzo.

"Why did they have the sheet pulled over my face?" Helen asked when she saw her beloved husband, Lorenzo.

"When I woke up, the sheet was all over, and it covered me completely," she declared.

He could tell she was worried, scared, and a little agitated. "I don't know why, my love," Lorenzo said. "But whatever they thought honey, it is not happening today." He was certain Helen's doctors were misdiagnosing her and not providing the proper care to their Black patient. "The doctors called me while I was at work'; that's why I'm here my love. They told me you had passed." They laughed hysterically about the incident, and then he took her home.

Later, within the same month, Helen was sick again. This time, the doctors wanted to do an experimental type of medical treatment. They wanted Lorenzo to sign a proclamation giving the doctors the right to surgically open her skull and examine her brain. They claimed they wanted to determine what was happening to her brain to cause her distress. Lorenzo told them there was no way he would allow it without discussing the procedure with the entire team of three or four doctors.

"Are you going to cure her?" Lorenzo asked them. "Will she be alright?"

"We cannot promise anything," the doctors replied. "However, we can use her issue as a medical experiment so that we will know how to save other lives in the future."

Lorenzo became exceptionally distraught. How dare they ask him to use his beautiful and loving wife, Helen, as a guinea pig! "No way… No!" Lorenzo said to himself. "When God gets ready to take her, it will not be because the doctors were experimenting on her. No, I cannot, I will not…No way!"

Helen's medical team told Lorenzo that the climate was too extreme in Boston and advised him to take her to a warm climate where the temperature was more constant to ease her condition. After listening to the doctors, Lorenzo decided that he and his wife would leave Boston. Nothing meant more to him than Helen, and to help reduce her suffering and improve her quality of life, he knew they had to leave. So, Lorenzo and Helen headed back to El Dorado, Arkansas.

Before the winter of 1947, Lorenzo packed up his family and headed to El Dorado, Arkansas. He wanted to avoid Boston's extreme weather and brutal winters. Helen's parents, Erma and Moses, were overjoyed to have their only child back home again and to see their new grandson and son-in-law. Lorenzo and Helen realized shortly after they arrived in El Dorado that Helen was pregnant again. They decided that Lorenzo should go to San Diego, California, where Lorenzo's parents and siblings had relocated from Texas. Years earlier, he had sent his parents money from his military allotment to help them relocate. He knew that opportunities for work in San Diego were much greater than in El Dorado. It was best that Helen stayed in the care of her parents and former doctors during her pregnancy. After the birth of the baby, Lorenzo would come back to El Dorado and pick up Helen and their two children.

On March 12, 1948, their second son was born, Robert Charles Pitts. It was said that Robert was the first Colored baby to be born in the maternity ward of Warner Brown Hospital in El Dorado, due in part to the fact that Helen's mother and father worked for one of the richest families in El Dorado. The hospital opened in 1921 at a cost of $300,000.00. It was financed by Paul Brown, a renowned local businessman. The hospital was named in memory of Paul Brown's father, Warner Brown. During the 1940s in El Dorado and across the country, Colored children were delivered by a midwife at home.

Lorenzo found employment immediately after arriving in San Diego. He lived with his parents in the house that he helped his parents purchase after helping them pay off debts stemming from the family's years of sharecropping in Texas, a requirement before the family could leave the State of Texas. Months later, Lorenzo purchased a late-model automobile, large enough for his family to ride comfortably on their trip to California. The time had come for Lorenzo to return to El Dorado to pick up his wife and two sons, his family.

3

HELEN: "THE PROMISE"

Taped recollection of Lorenzo Pitts, Sr.

Sonny, it is not easy for me to persistently record my memories on these tapes without my mind receding to the many years ago when you were so small and so young, but we had responsibilities to you as our first-born son, although we have two children. I am beginning to think about your mother, Helen, at this moment. The death promise that I was given was asked to do, promised that I would do. I always wanted to try to complete any job that was given to me. I wanted to do this job so good that the living, or the yet-to-be-born, couldn't do it any better. I often wondered what other responsibilities and how long God was going to give me while I am here on this earth. I want to be able to do something distinct enough that you and Robert can understand, the kindest individual, the kindest person, the loving individual person that your mother really was.

I can assure you, well, at least in my opinion, Helen did not want to leave her family so soon. But God had a plan for her, and He has sent an angel down to conduct one of his instructions.

I still feel strongly that Helen pleaded to God in her final moments, saying, "Oh Lord, I will go. I will leave my two children and my husband. But I want to ask if you would let me do one thing. I want to let my family know that the time has come for me to leave, and Lorenzo must have the sole responsibility to raise our two children."

I can imagine her saying, "Just allow me that chance."

My mind returned to the day that changed my life forever. I had to leave my job and come home that afternoon. Helen was sitting upright in the bed with her back against the headboard. She was cheerful despite her illness.

The room was quiet, but she said, "Lorenzo, I knew you were coming. I knew you would be here. I have something I have got to tell you. Something that I want you to promise me."

I began to get a little nervous. I did not know. And then she said, "You must tell me that you will take care of our two boys."

Again, I recall, as if it were just yesterday or today. I said, "Helen, you don't feel very well. Why don't you take a nap? Relax and rest."

She looked at me and smiled. I went over and sat on the side of the bed. She laid over in my arms and looked up at me, sincerely as one could be, and said to me, "Lorenzo, you got to promise me."

The sun was shining through the window. It's the way the house was laid out, and the sun was setting in the west, and she said, "We don't have much time. Lorenzo, please promise me, please promise me that you will not give our two boys to your mother, nor will you give them to my mother to raise. You must raise them. It is your responsibility. Please promise me."

At first, I was hesitant to make such a promise because it just did not sound right. Something was wrong. Why would such orders be given to me because she was such a good mother, a loving mother, and one that cared so much for her children? But, I realized that this was an unusual request. And she repeated it to me again.

She said, "You have to promise me, please promise me."

Those were her last words on this earth, in this life. And I recalled, it was so clear, so plain to me right now.

And I told her, "Yes, Helen, I will raise our two boys."

And she said to me, "Complete the sentence. I want to hear from you. We don't have much time now."

I said, "Yes, I will raise them. I will not give them to my mother, neither will I give them to your mother. I will raise them myself."

Then, she looked up at me, eyes so wide and clear, and I held her in my arms, holding her tight. And she smiled. She laid back in my arms, and God took her at that moment. At that moment, I realized that she had gone, that she had left. And her last words were concern about her children. Yet, I often wonder what really went through her mind. But one thing I can say is that she never, never quibbled or attempted to take back anything she said or attempted to change her mind about what she was requesting in her last moments on this earth.

I am so pleased that God made it possible for me to be the one and the only one there with her at the time He took her. There is something that I will never be able to understand. But I do believe, I do believe that she knew her time was up on this earth.

I would not dare to overwhelm her with questions during that time, though I had so many to ask. I never knew whether she wanted me to ask questions, sit and talk, or just quietly comfort her in those moments. I will never know. She wanted God to give me some vision or sign so that I could fully understand her wishes. And I would have responded a little differently, provided better comfort or shown my true raw feelings. I should have pleaded, "Helen, please don't go." However, I do not know if she wanted me to say that and revealed distress during her final moments.

Regardless of what I might've wondered in those final moments, I strongly believed God had His plans, even when man has no direction, no concern, no need to speculate, no need to contemplate, and no need to try to change God's will. Because when God's plans are in motion, those plans will not deviate. Sonny, I am not able to continue right now… I hope you understand.

4

EARLY MEMORIES OF SONS

Taped recollection of Lorenzo Pitts, Sr.

Sonny, do you remember when I used to take you and Robert with me to my job? As you grew older, you boys would learn about the business while doing your homework and/or study. Sometimes you would take a nap while I was working. That time was also when things were not particularly good at home. You boys were mistreated by my second wife, your stepmother. I have no problem admitting it now you were ill-treated, and I'm sorry. My heart was tremendously saddened about the entire ordeal.

Lorenzo reiterated the numerous times he prayed and asked God to help him. "Help me in some way so that I can feel comfortable in my own mind and that I am doing what Helen asked of me," he would ask of God.

Remembering and repeating himself, "She asked for so little when she was here on this earth," he said as he evoked Helen's memory. "She was so comfortable with so little. She was never the type of person who wanted a lot. She was never someone who nagged." Helen was comfortable with the quiet, small, and simple things in life. The simple things most people would not find satisfaction in, Helen enjoyed.

That trait in Helen meant so much to Lorenzo, more than she knew before her untimely passing. After Helen's death, Lorenzo was unable to fully enjoy his life until a few years later.

I feel blessed that God made it possible for me to meet someone as special as your mother, Helen."

There were often times you never knew my heart was so broken due to your mother's passing because I was relentlessly working, and you and I were routinely working together. Do you recall Ms. Downy, who used to take care of you? She was a breath of fresh air for me during those challenging times, and we had fun together. We would laugh and talk. Do you remember those days? I am sure you remember."

Sonny, it is not easy for me to continue to discuss it, but I cannot help but mention again that Helen wanted so little, and she asked me to do the one simple thing during her last breath on this earth, and she mentioned her children, her boys. She said to me, "You have a responsibility, and I do not want you to give up on your responsibility. Promise me."

I can assure you, well, at least in my opinion, Helen did not want to leave her family so soon. But God had a plan for her, and He has sent an angel down to conduct one of his instructions. I still feel strongly that Helen pleaded to God in her final moments, saying, "Oh Lord, I will go. I will leave my two children and my husband. But I want to ask if you would let me do one thing. I want to let my family know that the time has come for me to leave, and Lorenzo must have the sole responsibility to raise our two children." I can imagine her saying, "Just allow me that chance."

Sonny, this is an area where I have asked myself repeatedly whether I am happy with life. I found myself unable to continue because I don't know whether I am happy or sad, or if I am lonely, or even disappointed in myself for not being able to understand what Helen was trying to tell me in her last words. But one thing for sure, there are times my heart gets so heavy. I remember back to the time when I arrived home from work, she told me, "I knew you were coming." That is a powerful statement. I knew you were coming. In that moment, I knew I was needed. She started talking. That is when she said to me, she said, "I do not have much time." That is the reason that in my mind, I do believe that she had a little talk with God and asked God to give her a little more time. And asked God to communicate to her husband. I am not able to tell you, or able to tell Robert, why I was supposed to come home that day. But I do believe a strong, strong belief, that there is a God in Heaven. He is there, He created man in His own image. He giveth and He taketh. That is one of the areas where I get some comfort, knowing too that God was with Helen. God had spoken to her. God had let her know that He has a place for her, and her time on this earth, that He created, was finished. That she must come home. Come home and continue to do the job that He has for her to do, beyond, beyond man's interpretation. And there is when I think she realized that her husband needed to be warned.

El Dorado

Taped Recollection of Lorenzo, Sr.

Sonny, this is an area where I am sure you will be as concerned about as I was at that time. When we finally arrived in El Dorado from California, there was a solid worry and a heavy load, a weight, like an anchor in my heart down to the bottom of the ocean. The fact is. I did not know what ailments Helen had. All I had to go on, God giveth. and He taketh in His own good time.

I asked the funeral parlor if they could make arrangements to get an autopsy report on the body. I wanted to know if they could tell what caused Helen's death. They told me, yes.

I said, "Do that!" So, that's when they came up with the direct cause, and I asked him to be fair to me. I asked them to spell it out in plain language so I could understand what my wife was suffering from, and the things that she was being treated for. I just did not understand.

And they told me that she had what you would call an acute attack. I recall the word just as if it were spoken moments ago. I said, "Spell it out. What is that?"

"Acute attack means that the main artery leading to her heart, the blood vessel, burst, and that is the cause of her death."

I asked them, "Is this something that just happens?"

He said, "No, it is something that's possible," and then repeated, "Possibly something she was born with. Her heart was small and weak, and it burst. That was the cause. She did not have a heart attack. This was just something that had to happen and did happen."

I said, "Ok."

I was somewhat satisfied with the statement and with the answers that were given to me at that time. Now, this took place before the funeral because I wanted to know....I wanted to know. Therefore, nothing in the world could have pleased me anymore. The best thing I would have wanted was to have Helen with me. To have Helen with us. But since God had other plans, I wanted to

From Sharecropper to Multimillionaire

know what man had to offer, trying to satisfy my mind. I looked over the molehill into the mountains, and I looked directly in the east and said, Oh God, give me strength. I have a job to do. Let me be able to do the job. I will make every effort. If there comes a time that I will fail, please accept my apology. I will continue to try and try to do better.

I will always remember I have an obligation. I had a promise, what we would call a 'death promise.' Those were the last beautiful, sweet-sounding words that Helen asked me to do. She said, and she repeated it; I made that promise that I would take care of her and our two children. I had no choice. You and no one would ever know the sleepless nights and days that I have had and did have. Even when I looked happy, I might have been crying inside. Even when I looked like I was joyful, I might have been sad. Many days, many days, I asked God why me? Why put this heavy burden on me?

Erma Lucille Heard and Moses Lewis Heard migrated to El Dorado in the 1920s from Dubach, Louisiana. Erma and Moses were hired by the Bebe family. Erma was hired as a housekeepe and Moses as a handyman and outdoor worker. They both became loyal and efficient workers for more than fifty years, working longer than today's retirement age of 65. Like most domestic workers in the South, there were little or no retirement benefits forthcoming from their employers, regardless of the years of service. But over the years, Moses and Erma managed to acquire a small house with the help of the Bebes. They also were able to put away some funds to help them when they were no longer physically able to work and had to retire.

El Dorado, Arkansas, became known as a 'boom-town' when oil was discovered just outside of the city in 1921, fifteen miles from the Louisiana border, marking the beginning of commercial oil production in Arkansas. In the decades following the discovery of oil, El Dorado grew by leaps and bounds. The population catapulted from 4,000 to 25,000, and many oil-related businesses, including commercial rail travel, were established. The Bebe family business was one of the new establishments. Their business provided products and supplies to oil speculators and oil field operators. It wasn't long before the Bebe family became rich and part of El Dorado's high society.

After Helen Lucille Heard's Homegoing and burial services, Lorenzo and his sons took up residency with Helen's parents. This was a period of bereavement, bonding, caring for toddler Lorenzo, Jr., 2-year-old, and 4-month-old baby Robert, and finding a sense of well-being and stability for the family. The toddlers brought much happiness and healing to the grief-stricken family.

Erma secured work for Lorenzo with her own employer. She was a housekeeper of long-standing spanning three generations for one of the richest families in El Dorado, the Bebe family (daughter Wallace and granddaughter Luttrell), working tirelessly for mother, daughter, and granddaughter.

With Erma's recommendation, Lorenzo acquired the job of chauffeur. It was not his dream job, but he needed the job to support his boys and save up enough money to go back to Boston as soon as the boys were older. Lorenzo always wanted to be in business for himself, and he thought Boston provided the best opportunities. Years before, he helped his family leave sharecropping in Texas, and he wanted no part of the racist South but knew he needed help with the boys until they were older.

Lorenzo chauffeured the Bebe family members around El Dorado in their late-model limousine. He was always dressed appropriately and looked immaculate in his chauffeur uniform and hat. It wasn't long before people took notice, particularly in the "Bottoms," the section of town known as the "Colored" section. Erma and Moses lived in the "Bottoms" when they first arrived in

El Dorado from Louisiana. They lived in a small wooden house down the street from the poultry factory and across the street from the Mount Calvary Baptist Church. Everybody knew everybody! And everybody knew all of the "goings-on."

Several months after he started chauffeuring, he met Roselee Ridgell, a slim-framed, fair-complexioned, alluring, and spirited young El Dorado native. She told Lorenzo that she knew Helen, which was very comforting to him. He was still wrestling with grief from Helen's premature death, anxiety from the death promise he made to Helen, the responsibility of raising their sons, working a job without a future, living with his in-laws, and most of all, living back where he had escaped from just a few years ago, the Jim Crow South.

He continued to see Roselee, and it wasn't long before they became intimate. The relationship was consummated, and an understanding was forged between the two of them. He would take Roselee with him to Boston, fulfilling her dream to get out of the "Bottoms and the South," and she would help with the care and raising of his boys. They married in December of 1949. Soon thereafter, Lorenzo, Roselee, Lorenzo, Jr., now 4, and Robert, 2 years of age, were on the train headed to Boston.

Lorenzo, Jr. said, "Riding the train was the first experience that I retained as a memory from my childhood. The sounds and the happenings I experienced on the train stayed with me all my life."

5

WORLD WAR II NAVY BUDDY

Shortly after he returned to Boston, Lorenzo caught up with his World War II Navy buddy, Thomas Middleton. Middleton was overjoyed to see Pitts, who had always treated him like a brother since they met during the War. The two friends from the South (Texas and South Carolina) had served their country, and now that Pitts had returned, it was time again to put their heads together to see how they could build a successful life in Boston.

Thomas Middleton was born and raised on James Island, a town in Charleston County, South Carolina. Fort Sumter, the site of the first battle of the Civil War, is located on an island just off the eastern tip of James Island. The Island was largely agricultural, with Sea Island cotton forced-labor farms covering much of the Island. Growth accelerated after World War II, and James Island became a suburban bedroom community to Charleston.

He enlisted in the Navy in 1940, after he was sent to a "forced-labor work farm" and relegated to farm work after completing school. He thought that he was going to be sent to a trade school.

He told his sister, "I'm not going back after the Christmas break."

His sister told Thomas, "If you don't, you better have a job."

From Sharecropper to Multimillionaire

He said, "That's why I went and signed right up."

While he was taking a correspondence course to become an electrician, the Navy contacted him. After basic training, they told him that his job was to wait on the White officers, make their beds, and shine their shoes.

He said, "Heck, I didn't do that at home."

He didn't want to get a BCD (Bad Conduct Discharge), so he signed up for 6 years and was assigned to the USS Ellis, a four-stacker used for beach landings. Middleton didn't want to be labeled 'queer' like some of the other men in his community who took a BCD and returned home early.

He said, "We went to England, Northern Ireland, and any place on the Atlantic coast." The ship was in Nova Scotia when the War broke out in December 1941. He had been in the Navy for about 3 years when he was transferred to the Francis M. Robinson 220, Destroyer Escort, where he met Pitts.

Pitts was a second-class Steward. A Steward was one of the few jobs that Blacks were allowed to work in during the War. Blacks were assigned to non-combat units and relegated to service duties such as supply, maintenance, and transportation.

Middleton said, "I stayed on that ship, Pitts and I stayed on that ship. He was rated. He was a second-class steward. That's a lot of money. You know what I'm referring to. I've been on other ships, but I've never seen anyone as young as he is in second class. I said, how the heck did he get to rank like that? He must say, 'Yessir.' That's what I said to myself that he must be saying, 'Yessir.' You know, that's how we had to get a rank back then. That's what I was thinking in my mind, so I started saying 'Yessir,' too."

A friendship to last a lifetime was in their future. After the War, they both spent many years enjoying the company of other veterans as members of the VFW (Veterans of the Foreign Wars), in Boston.

They always referred to one another by their last names, the 'Navy way,' Pitts and Middleton. They each had married the love of their life while they were serving in the Navy. After Pitts was discharged in October of 1945, they found a large house in Boston, and the two young couples started living together, each paying half of the rent. Middleton said he was working nights, 11pm to 7am.

One evening, when his wife Theresa called out, "Tommy, get up! Helen fell out here."

It was about 8:00 pm. Theresa was in the kitchen when she heard a noise. Helen had been sitting nursing Lorenzo, Jr., 'Sonny.' The house had a little oil burner, and she was sitting near it. She had passed out, knocked the heater down, and dropped the baby.

Middleton said, "I ran back into my room, got the cover that had been covering me. My wife was picking up the baby and covering Helen. I put the fire out and then reported it. We called Pitts at work and told him about the incident."

To Thomas and Theresa Middleton, Lorenzo and Helen Pitts were not just friends but like family. They were extremely concerned about Helen's health problems and reassured their friends, the Pitts, had their support during this critical time. Sometime after Helen's medical incident, taking her doctor's advice, Lorenzo and Helen left Boston and headed to El Dorado, Arkansas, Helen's hometown with a warmer climate, and into the arms of welcoming and caring parents.

A couple of years later, when Lorenzo returned to Boston in 1950 after Helen's death, Middleton and Pitts reconnected and remained friends throughout their lives, supporting one another. Middleton's sons, Thomas, Jr. (Tommy), Roger, and daughter Gloria, befriended Lorenzo, Jr., and Robert. Middleton and Pitts engaged in business enterprises, civic and social affairs, and became active members of the Veterans of Foreign Wars (VFW) in (Roxbury) Boston. Middleton became an exceptional golfer and was an original member of the Boston Pro-Am Golf Club. The Club members held golf clinics in neighborhood schools, introducing and teaching local children about the game of golf.

In 1958 and 1959, Thomas Murray Middleton, Sr. became the first African-American to be awarded Franklin Park Golf Course's

'Club Champion of the Year Award', and in 2004, he was honored for his accomplishments in a ceremony at Boston City Hall.

When Middleton's son Thomas (Tommy) Murray, Jr. passed away from injuries resulting from a car accident in New York on April 10th, 1971, at the age of 25, and son Roger passed away nine days later, on April 19th, 1971 from injuries he sustained in the same car accident, at the age of 24, his friend Pitts was there to provide hands-on care and emotional support to his friend Middleton and his family.

When Middleton's wife, Theresa Mae Wright Middleton, passed away in James Island, South Carolina, in 2007, his dearest friend Pitts and his sons Robert, Lorenzo, Jr. (and wife Claudia) were there to provide love and support to Middleton, better known as Uncle Thomas, and his daughter Gloria.

After a lingering illness, Thomas Murray Middleton passed away on August 1st, 2015, at the age of 96, at home and under the loving care of his daughter, Gloria, in Dorchester (Boston), Massachusetts.

6

A NEW BEGINNING

Roxbury was founded by English colonists of the Massachusetts Bay Company in 1630. Roxbury was a key location during the Revolutionary War, particularly for land-going traffic to Boston. It led the nation in the fight for independence. It was also home to abolitionist William Lloyd Garrison after the Civil War. Its colorful history includes the early settlers and colonists, who included John Ruggles and John Eliot. By the 19th century, it became an industrial town with a large community of English, Irish, and German immigrants. In the Mid-19th century, there was a growing Jewish community. An expanded trolley-car and elevated rail systems helped the Dudley commercial area of Roxbury, called Dudley Square, flourish. Department stores, furniture stores, theaters, and other retail establishments gave life to the neighborhood, including jazz nightclubs. Over the years, the population changed from Irish immigrants to Jewish. In the 1950s and 1960s, the neighborhood changed from a neighborhood of White residents to predominantly non-White people. Like many other urban areas across the country, Black people migrated to Boston from the rural South, seeking economic opportunities and better living conditions, and an escape from racial violence and the ills of segregation.

Roxbury was the center of the Black community in Boston. Numerous migrants from the South came seeking a better way of life. Over time, Roxbury evolved from a rural neighborhood of Boston into an industrial community and a city with an urban feel, with many restaurants, coffee shops, bars, and parks. The majority of residents rent their homes or apartments. Public schools are above average; many families and young professionals appear more liberal in their ideology.

In the late 1960s and 1970s, Roxbury underwent significant changes due to urban renewal and land acquisition by the Commonwealth for the expansion of Interstate Highway U. S. I-95. "The proposed Southwest Expressway, an extension of I-95, faced significant opposition and was scrapped, but not before causing extensive displacement and destruction in Roxbury and surrounding neighborhoods. Thousands of homes were razed, and businesses were demolished in preparation for the highway, including areas like Roxbury Crossing and Jackson Square, and neighborhoods like Fort Hill suffered severe abandonment.[19]

Today, Boston and the greater Boston Metropolitan area have great institutions of higher education and famous historical landmarks: Harvard (Cambridge, founded in 1636, the oldest university in U.S.), Massachusetts Institute of Technology (Cambridge, founded in 1861), Tufts (Medford, founded in 1852), Northeastern University (Boston, founded in 1898), and Boston College (Boston, founded in 1863), to name a few. The John F. Kennedy Presidential Library and Museum is also located in Boston. Urban regeneration, restoration, and renovations, such as Boston Common, America's first public Park, and the new Greenway Park, continue to occur. The expansion of liberal ideology has helped lead the way to the legalization of same-sex marriage and the enactment of healthcare reform. For nearly 100 years, Boston has been home to many major professional sports teams, such as the Boston Red Sox (1921), Boston Bruins (1924),

Boston Celtics (1946), New England Patriots (1959), and numerous other sports teams.[2]

After World War II, many veterans and their families decided to make Boston their home. Lorenzo, Sr, and many of his cohorts had the same mindset. Leaving the South behind, they were ready to start a new beginning and were open to Boston's opportunities.

Many veterans who decided to make Boston their new home looked forward to accessing the services and benefits under the 'Servicemen's Readjustment Act of 1944,' signed into law by President Franklin Delano Roosevelt on June 22, 1944. Today, the bill is commonly known as the 'G.I. Bill.' The benefits offered under the G.I. Bill include education, home, farm ownership, and business opportunities. More than eight million WWII veterans went to school and utilized their G.I. Bill benefits between 1945 and 1956.[3]

Though the benefits of the bill were open to all veterans, Jim Crow-era discrimination prevented Black veterans from receiving the same opportunities as their white counterparts, and Boston was no exception. The years and generations have widened this wealth gap and magnified the struggles that many Black Americans face today.

Many Black veterans talked about the discrimination they saw while serving and upon returning home, and the difficulties they faced when trying to obtain health care and other benefits from their local Veterans Affairs offices. Service members, both Black and white, put their lives on the line for their country during the war, but unlike white veterans, Black veterans faced open hostility from the society they had helped to preserve.[12][4]

When Lorenzo and Rosalee arrived in Boston in January 1950, winter was in full bloom, with short days and frigid temperatures day and night. It was normal winter weather for Boston. Rosalee was a new bride, born and raised in the South, and didn't find the harsh weather welcoming. She was a young woman of 18 years in a strange city, much bigger and busier than El Dorado. The city was experiencing rapid post-war growth, and business opportunities abounded. Lorenzo and Rosalee wanted to be a part of the new growth. Rosalee set out to turn their small apartment into a home in Roxbury. She was no longer in the 'Bottoms,' and El Dorado was more than 1,500 miles away. She was married. Roxbury was a new start and the beginning of a dream she had nurtured as a young girl.

Lorenzo worked hard to establish a painting and wallpaper business. He worked long hours, traveling many miles, taking public transportation, carrying buckets of paint, rolls of wallpaper, supplies, and even ladders to his customers' homes throughout the Boston Metropolitan Area, until he could purchase a used station wagon. Lorenzo enrolled in a chemistry course at a local college to research and understand paint's chemistry and help him expand his business opportunities. No known information is available regarding whether Lorenzo successfully accessed the G.I. Bill's educational benefits to help him academically.

The young couple's marriage was filled with challenges from the beginning. Their first child was born on February 1, 1950, less than two months after they arrived in Boston. However, Lorenzo was determined to provide a respectable living and good housing in a safe neighborhood for Rosalee, Lorenzo Jr., Robert, and their new baby daughter, Katherine. Several years into his residency in Boston, Lorenzo, his Navy buddies, and business colleagues Thomas Middleton and Reese collaborated to purchase two three-story, six-flat brick connecting apartment buildings at 189-191 Walnut Avenue in Roxbury, built in 1940. Lorenzo and Rosalee lived on the second floor in the 191 building. Their spacious six-bedroom apartment had plenty of room for their growing family. And grow it did.

No known information is available regarding whether Lorenzo, Middleton, and Reese successfully accessed G.I. Bill veteran Home and Business Ownership benefits to help them in their homeownership and business pursuits. But we do know that they continued to press forward to build a better life for their families and themselves than the life they left behind, despite the barriers and obstacles they faced. The purchase launched their careers in the apartment and housing market.

With their family's continued expansion and growth and Lorenzo's extended working and school hours, the couple struggled to make their marriage work. In 1957, Erma, the mother of Lorenzo's late wife, came to visit her only grandchildren, Lorenzo Jr. and Robert. It had been years since she had seen the boys. She hadn't seen them since they left El Dorado in December of 1949, when the boys and Lorenzo stayed with her and Moses after Helen's death and burial. Helen was their only child, and she and Moses dearly missed their grandchildren.

A day or two into Erma's visit, Lorenzo Sr. and Rosalee had a dispute and confrontation when he came home from work early one afternoon. The disagreement resulted in Erma abruptly cutting her visit short, leaving with her two grandsons and luggage in hand. She requested Lorenzo to drive her and her grandsons, Lorenzo, Jr., and Robert, to the Greyhound bus station, and he complied. They boarded the first bus to El Dorado, Arkansas, more than 1500 miles away from Roxbury and Rosalee.

Return to Roxbury

The spirited boys enjoyed being at their grandparents' home. It was a definite life change for the boys, who were used to living in an apartment in Roxbury. Farm life was a dramatic difference from city life. It was also a big challenge for Moses and Erma to parent two high-spirited boys, ages 11 and 9, while fulfilling their work responsibilities to their employer, the Bebe Family.

After a taxing but joyful, heart-warming, and heart-healing stay for two years, their frolicking in the country ended. No more chasing chickens around the chicken house and the farmhouse, playing with Pup and the other dogs, or feeding the calves, General McArthur and General Eisenhower, to prepare them to be slaughtered. No more attending spirit-filled Mount Calvary Missionary Baptist Church with Grandma Erma. No more experiencing what it's like going to an all-Black segregated school or shopping at the Piggly-Wiggly Grocery store with Grandma Erma. No more rides in Grandpa Moses's open-back truck or experiencing exciting adventures on the farm with him. No more learning the proper behavior for Black children that they must adhere to if they are to live and survive in Arkansas and the South. Those rules were taught and reinforced daily by Grandma Erma and Grandpa Moses. Their father had arrived.

Lorenzo had come to El Dorado to take his sons back to Roxbury/Boston for the 1959 Fall School Term. At first, the boys were gleeful when their dad drove up in his car. They thought he had come to visit, but they soon learned that he was taking them back to Roxbury to live with their stepmother, Rosalee, again. What they didn't know was that their father was trying to fulfill the "death-bed promise" he made to their mother, that he would raise their sons, and that he wouldn't give them to his parents or her parents to raise.

Things didn't go well between Rosalee, Lorenzo, Jr., and Robert. The two-year absence did little to improve their relationship. It didn't take long before the dissension between her and the boys, which had been present before they left for Arkansas, worsened.

When Lorenzo Sr. came home from work one evening, the hostile atmosphere in the house was such that he knew that the boys could not live in the same house as Rosalee. He immediately found them a home and surrogate mother to help him raise Helen's boys ... his sons. Mrs. Willetta Downey, their new surrogate mother, was a widow and mother of two senior high school teenagers, one boy and one girl.

In the following years, ten children were born to Rosalee and Lorenzo Sr. and raised in their sometimes unhappy and often dysfunctional home environment. The couple was worn down and exhausted. Numerous pregnancies, parental burnout, unfulfilled expectations, and ongoing financial anxieties lead to much unhappiness and the death of hope for a brighter future together. After 23 years of marriage, Rosalee and Lorenzo divorced in 1972. In their divorce settlement, Lorenzo Sr. provided a small house, spousal support for Rosalee, and financial support for the children still attending school.

After an extended illness and a relentless battle with diabetes, which led to a double amputation of the legs, Rosalee Ridgell Pitts, second wife to Lorenzo Pits, Sr., mother of five girls and five boys, born in El Dorado, Arkansas, on November 14, 1931, passed away peacefully on February 13, 2005, in Boston, Massachusetts.

Out of respect for their twenty-three-year marriage and his love for their children, Lorenzo Sr. ensured that Rosalee's "Homegoing Services" were beautiful, dignified, and fitting tributes to a former wife, the mother of his ten children, and a Bostonian of 55 years.

Growing up in a dysfunctional family makes it difficult to recognize what is okay and not okay to tolerate in relationships. It is easy to believe that this dysfunction is normal, and it may feel comfortable to follow this path. At some point in our lives, we may start recognizing anxiety, stress, depression, and other emotions that come up for us when being around our family. Many dysfunctional behaviors repeat through generations; however, it is possible to break the cycle. It takes awareness and the willingness to set firm boundaries.⁵ *Selve 2021 McNulty, Moving Past Dysfunctional Families 09/07/2022*

Some characteristics of dysfunctional and toxic people may include acting harsh and critical, not showing concern for one's feelings or needs, calling derogatory names, refusing to compromise on anything, always having to be right, making unfair demands, not taking responsibility for their actions/blaming others, rarely saying they're sorry for something they have done, guilting or lying to get their way, and manipulating or taking advantage to gain control and to get what they want.⁶ *Reed 2021 McNulty, Moving Past Dysfunctional Families 09/07/2022*

Lorenzo Sr. Shares His Feelings

I thought about many things. What I will say now, I don't know why I feel this way, but what a mistake I made when I chose Rosalee. I thought that she would be a good mother, a substitute mother, because the fact is, she knew Helen. She knew Helen before I did. A little town in a small community; everybody knew everybody. However, everybody was never the same. Everybody did not think the same. Everybody had a different attitude, a different way they conducted themselves. But I often wondered why and what I did so wrong. I tried so hard to make the marriage last, but I could not, I could not. I'm talking about Rosalee and myself. I know she mistreated you and Robert so much. I prayed so many times, so many times, that she would not abuse you guys anymore, but I know she continued to do it. You can remember; I know you do. My sadness and my joy. During the times when you went to school, I tried to make it back to pick you guys up and take you to work with me. At least I know in my heart that I can say to Helen in a quiet voice, with no sound coming from my lips, but in my heart, I said, "Helen, I have our two boys with me. I have them with me. Please be satisfied, please be happy. Wait for us, please wait for us. We will meet again."

I believe this strongly. Sonny, I do believe. Sonny, I do believe this strongly that we will meet again. The four of us, the four of us, are going to meet again. I often wonder what a joyful time that will be. But whatever God has in store for us, we will accept it. But I want you to know, you might not ever think or ever give the thought that my heart was so heavy so many times until there were many times that I had to leave from you and Robert, because we as individuals, as human as we are, we have feelings, we can get hurt. I had to go to a quiet little spot, somewhere alone. And as I can say, as we little creatures would say, I will have a little talk with Jesus. I will have a little talk, ask Him to continually give me the strength to raise these two boys the way Helen would want me to do so. I don't understand why God took her, but I do know that He did take her away from us, left us alone, and we have struggled all of these years.

Now, in this late day in my life, I have thought about it so many times to put this on tape. And when you continued to ask me for it, I knew there were going to be things I would have to say and will say because I have to speak from my heart. I have to say what I feel. Every time I see you or Robert, you have to look over the molehill into the mountains, my heart skips a beat, and I have to think about Helen. For there is no way that I could ever forget. There is no way I could ever quit thinking about Helen because the fact is I don't know anyone; not too many individuals that have had a discussion with an individual that each one cared enough for each other so much. God had plans, and His plans were going to be fulfilled. And he let her know that she should tell me that she is leaving us. She had a job to do, also. So, that day will come again, that day will come again, that we will meet again. And we will be able to look at each other in the eye.

I often wonder if we're going to be able to understand. I ask God to forgive me if I have some shortcomings, and I have failed to comprehend or understand everything that she was trying to tell me. Maybe I should have, maybe I should have! But I have tried to remember in my own mind. Those few sentences are more than I am able to understand, break down, and explain to you and to Robert what it really meant to me. I have not sat down and talked to you and Robert this way, but many times I have wanted to.

My heart gets so full, and sometimes I can't, I cannot speak clearly. Like right now, it's not easy for me to do it, but I'm doing it with joy. I'm doing it because I owe this much to you. I owe this. It's no way that I can ask you or Robert to understand my feelings because the fact is you two boys were so young when God took Helen away from us. I don't believe you really remember her. The thing that you used to say to me, because you were only saying what I told you. You used to say to me, "Daddy, Mommy's sleep?" "Mommy's sleep?" And I used to tell you, "Yes, she will remain sleep. Yes, she is sleep."

Here is an area that I wanted to talk about a little more. The time we left California and brought her body to El Dorado to carry out one of the things that we talked about many times. That is an area where I keep thinking, why did we discuss our burial? Why? I don't understand it now. There were many times we discussed where we wanted to be buried. She once said to me, "I want to be buried in the cemetery not very far from the Homestead, where my mother and father live." I could stand on that front porch and look up at the hill, and I could see the grave in the cemetery.

We talked about it with so much joy, and we enjoyed talking about it. And I remember Helen said to me, "Where do you want to be buried?" I said, "I want to be buried next to you. We will be buried together." And I used to say, "Well, Helen, whoever leaves first, whoever dies first." She said, "No, you must make these plans. And I would like for us to be together, be buried together." I said, "That promise will go. We will be."

I will ask you, Sonny. Please, I hope it will not be too much for you. I hope I'm not asking for too much. I trust and hope, with all my heart, that you and Robert will find the time and understand how important this means to me. I'm asking you now, please, please, bury me next to Helen in the grave, wherever is near her. If possible, let my casket touch her casket. I know somewhere we will meet again and hold hands and laugh and talk. This is, um, perhaps, too much for me to ask, but at this moment, at this time in my life, I am not thinking about if it's too much now.

All I'm doing is racking my mind, going back into my thoughts about what we discussed. It's that early stage in our lives when we didn't have much time together. God knew how much time we had together, and why we had to make this one of the greatest and enjoyable topics. We talked about it. We laughed about it. There was no other, no other desire in our hearts. Neither one of us put death in front of us; we didn't look at it that way. Because we were young, and had so much living yet to do, so much, just so much to do. I know that I felt that we would live a long life together for a long time. But God had other plans. He knew, and He realized that He must take her away, that she will go and prepare such a place.

This is not an easy topic, but I can do it now. There were times I couldn't talk this way without breaking down with unforgettable thoughts. Sometimes my mind goes completely blank because I asked God, "Why did you take Helen? Why? Why Helen, not me?" Then, I said, "Oh God, forgive me because You knew what You were doing. Maybe that would've been too much for her if You had taken me first.

Sonny, I'm going to move on from that subject at this time. I cannot, I cannot state, at this time, that I will not talk about it more, or my mind and my heart will not act as if she were yet alive, cause I really enjoy talking about Helen. She was such a wonderful person. When I say Helen, I'm talking about your mother. Your mother was a wonderful person. We used to go to the church; you know the church. I believe it was called Mt. Calvary Baptist Church. She was pleased to go there. Now, that was her church. That was her mother and father's church. I went to what I will call my church. I think it was called Rock Island, the Methodist Church, because that's the church I belonged to. And we never discussed that much about one, or both of us, going to the other church. We went to both churches, and we served God together. And I can remember, as the preacher was preaching, there was so many times Helen just cried, tears running down her eyes. And she used to tell me, "Lorenzo, I am so happy. Lorenzo, I am so happy." And we spend this kind of time, sacred time, loving times after service. You know, in a country town like that, there would not be a Sunday when we wouldn't have a big dinner. We called it "Sunday dinner" after church service. There was always food to eat, food to give, food for company. Food for anyone. There was so much. There is so much I have yet to talk about.

Memories of the San Diego Family

Again, my mind goes back on something right now and I think it would be a most wonderful thing to bring forth right now. At the time, when my father was on his deathbed, I was not aware that he was leaving us at that time. I looked in his direction. He was looking directly at me. He called me by my name. I had a nickname that he had always called me for many years. He called me 'Speedy.'

My sister Beulah, who we called "Bee", and I were together that day at the hospital when my father decided to deliver something so powerful that at the time when he was telling me what to do, I was not able to understand and comprehend. I had no feeling that he was coming to the end of his life on this earth. But here is the thing that meant so much, the thing that rang out of his mouth, looking directly at me. He told me, "Go home and look for the praying hands. You are going to need them."

I recall that day as if it were yesterday or today. I responded and said, "Dad, why should I go and look for them? You can give them to me when you get home."

He looked at me, and he looked at Bee, and his words were, "I'm not going back home now. I am tired. I am tired. I will be leaving you."

At that time, Bee must have had a feeling. Some way, she must have felt the impact of a direct feeling, that voice was so clear, and she broke down and started to cry and said, "Oh Lord, help me."

I recalled, oh, what a wonderful moment that was. I went over, put my arms around Bee, and I said, "Bee, don't do that. Dad does not want sadness. He wants you and I to be pleased, be proud." We embraced each other, and we were able to control our feelings

And we went back into the hospital room where Dad was lying. He had his head up and was very alert. And I could not understand, as I would remember going back over the sentence, the statement that was made. I said, "Dad, earlier, you said you wanted me to have the praying hands. Why me? Why do you want me to have them?"

He said, and I'm going to quote his words, he said, "Speedy, you are going to need them. You must never, ever forget to pray. You are going to need the praying hands."

So, the subject died at that time while we were there. But later, as the time moved rapidly, it would come time for us to leave. Bee and I, we went back home, and we went into Dad's room. We went over and over that room with a fine-tooth comb. I was looking for a large something that could resemble the praying hands. We found nothing of that nature. Then we went back to check over the room, looking for something small. Something that we could feel Dad wanted me to have. But we found nothing.

The next day, it was time for me to leave and come back home to Boston. Oh, how wonderful it is. Even though my plan was to come back to visit again, but again God had plans. His plan was that Dad must leave us now. He had given me His final decision. He had given his final word, request, or I can say an order that He had given to me. And when I returned to Boston, there was a phone call that he had left. Then, I had to make arrangements to come back for the funeral.

As we went to the funeral, put our father to rest, and returned from the cemetery, I recall helping my mother walk up the little path, a few steps up the little path to and through the front door. The front door was the address of 2187 Everette Avenue. Mother had an old chair, I would say an old chair, her favorite chair that she sat in to watch television. The chair had 3 or 4 pillows on it. She felt that that would make her comfortable. My mother had a piano, one of those old pianos. As we crowded into the living room, I looked up. I looked at the piano. What stared me right in the face was the praying hands. I ran through the house and called for my sister Bee to come. "You and I is the only ones that had the grace of God to be there with Dad to hear his voice when he told me, 'Speedy, you must take the praying hands.' Here they are, here are the praying hands. It was right here in the house all the time. We were looking for them in the wrong place. If we can think back, we remember Dad never said the praying hands were in his room. He said in the house. He said in the house. We must get the praying hands; you must take them with you. You must keep them with you."

Sonny, I am a little heavy right now, my mind is reaching out again. There is another, a second death promise that I, that was given to me that I had to take. It must be a reason that I am not able to interpret the real depth of the real reason, but I can understand what it means to have something that you can depend on, you can hold onto. And that is something I hold on to. Sometimes, my heart gets so heavy, but I look over the molehill, into the mountains, and think about the praying hands. Then I say, "Oh God, help me. If it is thy will, let it be done." Sometimes, it's not easy. Sometimes the waves begin to shower, shake like a tree, the leaves on a tree, but I am still willing to go and try, and try to understand. Again, and again, I want to say, I am happy, I am pleased to have lived a good life up to this point. I am pleased and happy that I have had such a wonderful life. With all the trials and tribulations, I still feel that God has a place, a job for me to do. I want to do that job. I want to complete that job. I want to do whatever He might have for me to do. I am one of His little creatures on this earth. I will continue to work hard, be faithful, try to move forward, and do some of the things that God wanted me to do.

Lorenzo Sr. Speaks to Lorenzo Jr.

I'm going to try to talk about some of the other things in life, the other parts of my life that keep getting in the way right now, and I feel that I should talk about it. But I'm reluctant to mix the bad things in with so much good. Right now, I'm thinking about what I need to say, I'm asking myself, "Should I say it"? But I guess I should. I guess I should.

That time, when we left El Dorado to come to Boston. You were a little older then. You were old enough to know, and you could think for yourself, and you knew when something wasn't right. You knew when you were being mistreated as a person, and a lot of things were not good. They were not good. I have to say they were not good, cause I knew they were not good. And God knows I knew. I feel that He forgave me because I made a bad choice.

I did not make the choice intentionally. That was an error in my life that I made, and it's a checkmark there. I'm giving myself a grade, a rejection that I did wrong. But it wasn't intended to be that way. That was not the way. She (Rosalee) and I were two young individuals.

I can turn the pages back a little bit. As you guys were growing up, I'm sure you remember the lady called Mabel Chin—Ms. Chin, who lived in Chinatown. We used to do a lot of work down there. We used to work all day and late into the night, most nights. You guys would have a pallet laid down on the floor, and you would sleep. So, you would have your night's sleep. Although I felt that I didn't need much sleep, I felt that I needed to perform a service. I had family to take care of. I had another family at home.

There was one thing that you used to say. You were small and didn't understand, but you knew the difference, the difference between being treated nicely and being mistreated. You used to ask Ms. Chin, her name was Mabel Chin, you used to say, "Ms. Chin, why can't you be my mother?"

She would never answer you, and she'd come to me, and she said, "You know, the boys are so sweet. You are doing such a wonderful job with them. He keeps asking me why I can't be his mother."

And we'd laugh and joke about it. And I said, "Well, why don't you answer?"

She said, "I don't know how."

I said, "Well, if he ever asks me, I will explain it to him." But you never asked me, but you would continue to ask her.

She used to fix you guys' food and tell you, "Come on, sit and eat." I used to sit back and fight back the tears because there was no sadness at that time; there was happiness and joy. Seeing our boys, our two children. I'm speaking about Helen right now, Helen and me. Our two boys, being fed, nourishment, food flowing through their bodies.

I will recall so many times, so many times that you and I were together. We used to go to work together, work long hours together. We used to talk about what you wanted to be and what you wanted to do in life. I will never forget this particular time, one Saturday afternoon, we were doing a job in Brookline, and the job was nearly completed. I had to go downtown to collect a check so that we could do the things that people do on the weekend: cash the check, get money, go shopping, buy more material for the next job, or finish paying for the materials for the last job. Whatever it is. That was the thing that people did, and they still do that now. We make plans. We make preparations.

At this particular time, I had some screens and lumber I purchased, and I needed some work done. It was four cellar windows that needed to be reframed. And I knew, I felt I knew, but I didn't know nothing! I felt, and I thought I knew, because in school, you got an A+ in cabinet making. We used to do that work in school because it required measurements, arithmetic, adding, subtracting, multiplying, and fractions. You knew how to measure, and I said to you, "Do these windows, I have to run downtown. I'll be back."

You said, "Ok." I gave you the hammer, the nails, and the saw—all of the things you need to do the job.

When I returned, you had cut the lumber up, but you didn't have a single window done. When I returned, I said, "Sonny, you haven't done the windows." And you looked at me with that sincere look, and as you looked at me that way, I remembered how Helen was looking at me. I'm talking about your mother. And you told me at the time, you said, "Dad, I cannot do that work."

I said, "Why?' You have seen me do it."

You said, "Yes, but I can't do it. I tried." I said, "Okay. But you get an A+ in cabinet making."

And you said to me, "Yes, I remember when it comes to a test. I remember what I studied, and I remember the answers."

I recall I turned, and I started thinking. And at that time in your life, you were in your senior year in high school. And I asked you a question, I said, "Sonny, is it something that you really want to do? That you would enjoy doing?"

And you said, "Yes."

I said, "Okay, what is it?"

You said to me at that time, "It fascinates me when I see you change electric switches and outlets. Sometimes, you don't even cut the electricity off. I want to be an electronic engineer. I want to be an engineer."

I said, "Sonny, that's what you want to be?"

And you said, "Yes."

I said, "Okay. That is what you should be. You should be an engineer, an electronic engineer."

And that discussion never took place no more until after you finished school; then you wanted to go to Northeastern University, and you followed your education in that line. And I think about it now. You never veered; you never went too far away from that area. You always stayed in the engineering field. Strong individual. You know how to put together projects that one could not see how to do, but you were able to do it.

I remember when you were working at that place called Procter & Gamble that was at that soap factory near Quincy, and you were an engineer there. And you took me, walked me through, showed me the desk where you were working. You had diagrams with lines drawn on the paper. I look at them; they were so straight, so perfect. I felt extremely uplifted.

We went all around in different parts of the factory. I got an education, seeing so many different labels being put on different soaps. And that's when I realized that I was seeing all of the different soaps that were in the grocery stores, drug stores, corner stores, bars, and bars of soap. I was under the impression that every brand of soap was made at its own factory. But that particular manufacturer was making all of these different soaps under one roof and putting their own label on it. What an eye-opener that really was. I'm telling you, it was great.

Then you told me that they had a generator. The generator was huge. A size large enough to provide the energy that the big factory needed to turn all the machinery over; one generator was doing it. And you designed a generator one-fourth of the size of that particular one, and it put out more energy than that one would ever do. You saved hundreds and thousands of dollars for Proctor & Gamble.

I recall that you got very upset because you were in line for a great promotion because the knowledge that you had and used saved the factory thousands of dollars, but they did not give you the promotion. They gave it to someone else that you had trained and were still training. That person did not know the job, but they gave it to him. Not what he knew; it was who he was. That was the time you decided that you would quit because you felt that they had taken advantage of you. I guess I cannot complain about that because I do understand that feeling. That is a feeling that we have all suffered so badly, so wrong, so long as minority individuals. But, I have to look forward over the molehill and into the mountain and see how much you, as an individual, have accomplished. I can say I take my hat off to you, and let you know, even if you never knew before. I am so pleased and so happy that you went forward, and you went ahead, studied hard as you are still doing now, and became a great engineer. And also pleased to see you do the kind of work you're doing now. I turn the pages back in my mind, quick as a flash, and say, "Helen, our oldest son is doing what he wanted to do. He wanted to be an engineer. He wanted to go forward and do things which he wanted to do. This is so important."

I recall we had a long discussion. You were working in the business for a while, and we talked about where you wanted to go and what you wanted to accomplish. We discussed it, and that was the time you said that you wanted to go to Georgia, Atlanta, Georgia. I recall asking you why there, of all places. You stated very clearly, you said, "I have done research, and that is the place where I want to go, where a lot of my people are striving, looking forward, doing things, owning their own business, and it has Black colleges. Just so much is going on."

We discussed about you wanting to go to Georgia. I wouldn't dare discourage you. My thought was, and still is today, that's what you wanted to do; if that is where you wanted to go, you must go, you must do. I feel once you make up your mind about what you wanted to do, I believe you can do it.

I had to do that same type of thing. I had to make up my mind what I wanted to do in life. What kind of work I wanted to do. I wanted to be able to serve the public. I wanted to be able to serve all mankind. I wanted to be able to serve and help individuals that needed help. We all need help sometimes. But I wanted to help those who could not help themself. I want to be able to go into a business that I've chosen to do. I felt, in my mind, that this could be a year-round type of business. I didn't want to work for no one; I wanted to be the one that other people worked for. I wanted to be able to give jobs to every individual. I wanted to be able to train individuals in how to do work with their hands. The greatest tool that we can have in our life is our hands. This is a tool we use every day that God gave every man, every woman. And he also gave us five senses. Some of us use them to great advantage, and some of us don't do it well. Some of us make other decisions in life.

About my son Robert: I often asked myself whether there was another way to express the love I felt for both of you boys. I love you, Sonny, I love you and Robert very much. You have been such an achievement for me. It really hurts me to know that that I, our two boys,…one of them has chosen another way of life that is not necessarily positive. Sometimes I wonder what did I do wrong? Whether I failed Helen, and how did I fail her?

I have to say this right now. I'm thinking about my son Robert, your brother Robert. He made decisions I still do not understand why. It's no need for me to tell you or anyone that it bothers me; of course it does. Of course, it does! He had such an uplifted direction that he was going in. I thought he was going that way. I had no knowledge that he was falling by the wayside. I had no knowledge that he was involved with other individuals that would make him, encourage him, or entice him to another type of work; not work, but some other outlook on life.

He made a decision that he wanted to do certain things. I regret it, but I can't do anything about it. I didn't want it to be that way. I wanted both of you to do so much. But you are still working hard. And you made a statement to me here about six months ago; you asked me to quit worrying about Robert. Because the fact is, he made his decisions. You said, "Dad, you did not teach him how to do what he's doing now. He made that decision. Until he gets tired of the life that he's chosen to live, there's nothing you can do about it. Please do not listen to or get involved in his lifestyle. You let me handle it. I will take care of this type of situation, and in this type of situation, I know that you should not, under any circumstances, get involved. The kind of people hounding him would be coming to hound you, which would not be fair. You did not do that. I know you do not want that, but just let it go. You did not teach him how to do what he's doing now."

"I was very uplifted to hear you talk that way because the fact is there's no need for me to say, Well, it's okay now. It's okay now because I don't think about it that way anymore. I think about it in a different way. Different ways mean that I know I can understand right from wrong. I know that he did what he wanted to do. But whether that's what he wants to do or not, there's nothing I can do about it. And therefore, I must realize that I must take the backseat because the scripture is fulfilling."

> *"When I was a child, I spoke as a child, I understood as a child, I thought as a child: but when I became a man, I put away childish things"* 1 Corinthians 13:11

"So, until he quits acting like a child and acts like a man, I know he will be satisfied with himself. I just do not feel that he is pleased with the decisions that he has made, whether he made them on his own, or whether other people made them for him, or what other people hope he will make those decisions. I would never know. I would never try to know. I don't want to know. I question myself sometimes, where did I go so wrong? Why was I so unthoughtful or so dumb that I just couldn't see it? I just couldn't see a certain thing that was happening to him."

"Again, I should call a timeout and move away from that thought because that is not, it is not, the route that I wanted him to go. That is my son, who is my second son. We did all we could do; I felt that I did. Some decisions may not have been right, but I'm not sure. I do trust and hope that before, before the end of his life, he would look up and see the stars."

Our Plans vs God's Plans

Sonny, one day, everyone's time will come. We must try to live our lives the best way we possibly can. As mere mortal creatures, we must continue to understand that life is only given to us for a short time. I understand more now than ever before. Every day of our lives, we should try to live it to the peak and try to do what we can for humanity. Try to do what God wants us to do. And at this time in my life, I feel that I have made mistakes. I have made an error in choosing a mate I could live with and continue to raise my family after Helen. You know the whole story. The reason you know the whole story is because you lived it.

No one told you about the difficulties, trials, and tribulations we went through together. I wish there were a way I could remove all the pain and suffering that you and Robert went through because of my decisions. However, there is no way I can change the past. But I hope you and Robert will judge me by who I am as a person, not those difficulties. I have feelings, and I have compassion for every individual. I love working and spending time with people. I love children.

The Next Generation

I guess I can say I am somewhat near the end of my life. I have lived a long life up to this point. As humans, we all feel that our lives should last 100 years. But I am incredibly blessed that I have lived to enjoy 80 years of age. I feel wonderful, and my greatest joy is being able to visit you, Robert, and your children, grandchildren, and my great-grandchildren. Oh, what a wonderful, joyful feeling that was. I was able to spend time with four generations. Understand that it is truly unique that the firstborn is a male for four generations of the same family. That is something that a lot of people read about, and it is a rare occurrence.

I really enjoyed seeing how my grandsons work and how they succeed in life. I watched you from a distance, looking at the youngsters, and I understand how you felt during that moment because I felt the same as a father and grandfather. You were realizing that this is part of my lineage; this is a part of me. And you noticed that your sons are healthy, strong, and brilliant young men. There is no way that we cannot stand back with sincere pride, holding our heads high and praising God, "Oh God, thank you." I say it so often now, "Oh God, thank you for letting me live this long life. Letting me live to enjoy, to witness, to feel, and to be present to hold my great-grandchild. That is wonderful. That is so wonderful."

There is no other fitting response to sum up Lorenzo Pitts, Sr.'s life than the song **"My Way,"** sung by Frank Sinatra, songwriters Paul Anka / Gilles Thibaut / Claude Francois / Jacques Revaux.

We invite you to pause reading this book and enjoy the music and the lyrics at:
www.mywayFrankSinatraYouTube.com

Lorenzo Pitts, Sr. and Family

Helen Lucille Heard Pitts, Lorenzo Pitts   Lorenzo Pitts, Jr., Robert C. Pitts

Dr. Lorenzo Pitts, Jr., Lorenzo Pitts, Sr.

Lorenzo Pitts, Sr., Sister, Daughters, Daughters-in-Laws, Special Friendship

Lorenzo Pitts, Sr., Sons, Son-in-Law, Special Friendship

**Veterans of Foreign Wars (VFW)
Thomas M. Middleton, Sr.
And Lorenzo Pitts, Sr.**

**Theresa Mae Wright Middleton
Thomas M. Middleton**

Remembrance Lorenzo Pitts, Sr.
Sharecropper, WWII Veteran, Husband, Dad,
Entrepreneur, Philanthropist, Millionaire
August 13, 1924 -September 3, 2009

**Dr. Lorenzo Pitts, Jr.,
Thomas M. Middleton, Sr.
Departing graveside visit of**
Theresa Mae Middleton, St. James
Presbyterian Cemetery August 2014

2187 Everett Avenue, San Diego, California - Pitts Family's Home

The piano where the "Praying Hands" were found

Lorene, Beulah, Irene
Pitts Sisters

James, Lorenzo, Albert, Willie Ray, Napolean
Pitts Brothers

7

LORENZO PITTS, JR.'S LIFE HISTORY

Lorenzo Pitts, Jr. spent a lifetime working and living in and out of his father's shadow whenever he lived in Boston. He had a deep and abiding love for his father and tried hard to demonstrate that love. He never said or did anything that would disrespect his father or his memory. He admired him and would always go whenever he called and needed help with the business, no matter where he lived.

Lorenzo Sr.'s image loomed tall and broad among the residents in Roxbury, even though he was not quite six feet tall. His farm upbringing and Navy experience served him well. He was always about "taking care of business." He had taken up permanent residence in the city after returning in 1950 with a new bride after his first wife, Helen, died. This was a new start, a new beginning, and he was determined to make a go of it at all costs. He did not want to live in the Jim Crow South. He believed Boston was a growing city with many businesses and job opportunities, and his friend and cohort, Middleton, was there, but... There was always something that he could not shake, and it had to be considered at all times and any cost: the promise he made to Helen on her deathbed. "Yes, Helen, I will raise our two boys...I will not give them to my mother, nor will I give them to your mother. I will raise them myself."

The years living with their stepmother were agonizing for Lorenzo, Jr., and Robert. Lorenzo Sr. worked all day and evening to build a business and provide adequate housing and food for his family. As soon as the boys were in middle childhood, and whenever it was possible, they apprenticed under their father. He would pick the boys up after school and take them to work with him. Initially, they were responsible for putting down, picking up, and folding drop cloths and loading and unloading the work supplies. As they grew older, they assisted their dad with the wallpapering, mixing and applying the paste to the wallpaper for him to hang, baseboard trimming, and small construction. This continued until the boys completed high school. After finishing high school at age 17, Lorenzo Jr. enrolled in Northeast Institute of Industrial Technology. After completing his studies, he was certified as an Electronics Technician. It wasn't long after he graduated in December 1965 that Uncle Sam came calling. His country needed him. The Vietnam War was raging.

Lorenzo was drafted and sent off to Naval Station Great Lakes Boot Camp in Waukegan, Illinois, from August to November 1966. That same month, he returned to Boston and married his girlfriend and special love, Claire Thompson of Franklin, New Hampshire. Lorenzo and Claire met when Claire was a student at Chandler School for Women, established in 1883, in the Back Bay section of Boston. Chandler was a private professional training school that focused on training women in shorthand, typewriting, and the training of teachers. While attending Chandler, she lived at the Young Women's Christian Association (YWCA) on Berkeley Street. During the same period, Lorenzo was participating in Northeast Institute of Industrial Technology's Work-study Program, which allowed students employment opportunities to earn money while attending school. He worked in the kitchen at the YWCA. It wasn't long before they caught one another's eye in the cafeteria, and like magic, Lorenzo and Claire were attracted to each other. He thought she was untouchable. But she sent a message to him that she would like to date him. She was tall, slim, and built like a cheerleader. She was a striking young woman from a small town in New Hampshire with long brunette hair and deep brown eyes. Claire, the eldest of five siblings (three boys and two girls) of a prominent family in Franklin, was the first sibling to leave the nest. Her father was a judge and bank president, and her mother was a homemaker and socialite. Claire was raised to be the wife of a president, the first lady to a governor or mayor, the wife of a senator, or a successful business professional. But, on the sixth day of November, in the year of our Lord 1966, Claire married U.S. Navy Seaman Lorenzo Pitts, Jr. at St. Ann Episcopal Church in Dorchester, Massachusetts. Lorenzo Sr. was in attendance to provide parental support and permission to marry.

During Christmas military leave, the newlyweds moved to the Naval Great Lakes Training Center in Waukegan, Illinois, so that Lorenzo could attend electronics school. He completed the training and advanced to the Fire Control Technician Missile Third Class (FTM3) rank.

After his electronics training, he was sent to Vallejo, California, for missiles, radar, and computer training. Claire accompanied him and secured employment in the business administrative field while he was training. After completing his 2nd training phase, he advanced to the Fire Control Technician Missile Second Class (FTM2) rank and was assigned to the USS Long Beach Cruiser Guided Nuclear 9 (CGN9) at its home Port in Long Beach, California.

Lorenzo Jr. served in an integrated Navy, thanks to Executive Order 9981, signed by President Truman in 1948. The order mandated the desegregation of the U.S. military. "It is hereby declared to be the policy of the President that there shall be equality of treatment and opportunity for all persons in the armed services without regard to race, color, religion, or national origin." Lorenzo's dad, also a Navy man, had enlisted and served in the U.S. Navy from 1942 through 1945 as a Steward. Steward was the only occupation that Black people were allowed to hold during World War II, World War I, and all previous Naval battles.

After the birth of their son Derek on November 14th, 1967, Lorenzo Jr. was deployed to Vietnam in May 1968. Sometime after his second deployment, their second son, Jared, was born on April 10, 1971. After his birth, Claire experienced postpartum anxiety. The birth and care of her two children and a third military deployment scheduled for Lorenzo lay heavily on her mind. She exhibited anxious behavior, severe mood swings and appeared to be emotionally distraught. It became more difficult for her to provide proper care for the children. She began to have nightmares that Lorenzo would not return after his upcoming deployment. After many visits to her medical doctors and a psychologist, they determined it would be in the 'best interest' of the military if her husband was placed on inactive reserve status to serve out the remainder of his enlistment. The necessary paperwork was completed, and Lorenzo was put on 'inactive reserve status." He would no longer be deployed. He completed his tour of duty at the Port in Long Beach.

The family headed back to Boston by car in November 1971, stopping in El Dorado, Arkansas, so Claire could meet his grandparents, Grandpa Moses and Grandma Erma Heard. There were lessons in preparing Southern soul food, the ins and outs of farm life, and the endless 'fussing' over the boys. The visit was uplifting and a wonderful experience for Claire and the family.

During their marriage, the family took many trips, including a trip to Homer, Louisiana, to visit Aunt Avor Lee and Uncle Roy Henderson. The trips to El Dorado and Homer were extremely important to Lorenzo. His grandparents, aunt, and uncle provided a connection to his deceased mother, Helen. A connection that he always longed for and needed.

Family trips were made to Franklin, New Hampshire, to visit Claire's parents, Margaret and Judge Malcolm Thompson. Their interracial marriage had caused a break in their relationship. The visits helped to renew and strengthen the bond between daughter and parents, the acceptance of their new son-in-law, and the falling in love at first sight with grandsons Derek and Jared, toddlers.

In September 1972, he enrolled at Northeastern University and received a 5-year B.S. in Electrical Engineering. After graduating in June 1977, he worked with Procter & Gamble Manufacturing Company as a Production Supervisor in Quincy, Massachusetts. In 1982, his father was unwell and ordered by his doctor to take medical leave for at least one year. Lorenzo Jr. returned to Roxbury to help manage 1,000 units of affordable multi-family housing. He served as Lorenzo Pitts, Inc.'s (LPI) field supervisor.

In June of 1982, Claire, Lorenzo's wife, was diagnosed with cancer. Numerous tests and the latest treatments were pursued, but were unsuccessful. Claire was released home for Hospice care in December. It was a devastating and heart-wrenching period for the family. The boys and Lorenzo spent endless hours caring for and comforting Claire. The bond of love was so tight; it was as if love itself had the power to keep Claire with them. Six months ago, she was a doting, nurturing, and affectionate wife and mother. Somehow, she knew she had to love them enough to last a lifetime. After a tenacious fight, Claire passed away at home on January 30th, 1983, leaving behind grief-stricken, bewildered sons Derek, age 15, and Jared, age 12, her loving husband Lorenzo, and close family members to comfort one another. Claire was laid to rest in a cemetery in her hometown, Franklin, New Hampshire. This was an extremely stressful and heart-wrenching period for the family.

Just like his father before him, Lorenzo, Jr. had lost the first love of his life, and he was left to raise two sons without their mother, Claire, his beloved wife of seventeen years.

In 1983, Lorenzo Sr. ended his medical leave and returned to LPI. Over the next several months, Lorenzo Jr. completed his studies at Northeastern University's Graduate School of Business Administration in Boston. He was awarded a Master of Business Administration (MBA) degree in May 1983. He was recruited and accepted for a job with Corning Glassworks in Corning, New York, as a Product Engineer in the Telecommunications Division and assigned as an account manager for NASA's Space Shuttle Program. The boys spent their summer in rural Homer, Louisiana, with great-aunt Avor Lee and great-uncle Roy Henderson, immersing themselves in farm life. Lorenzo completed all the relocation issues in time for the boys to join him in Corning for the Fall school term.

In 1988, he returned to Boston to help his dad manage 1200 affordable housing units at Lorenzo Pitts, Inc. In 1992, he accepted a position with the MBTA (Massachusetts Bay Transportation Authority) as the first Black Engineer. He worked as a Technical Project Manager in the Bus Engineering Department. None of the MBTA's fleet of buses was air-conditioned. He initiated a demonstration project to retrofit many existing buses with "Thermo-King" air conditioning. After the project's success, MBTA, known as the "T" introduced a marketing campaign called "ICE-T." Thereafter, all new buses were ordered with air conditioning.

In 1994, he relocated to Atlanta, Georgia, and worked as an Adjunct Mathematics Teacher for DeKalb Technical College. In 2000, he was accepted and enrolled in Clark Atlanta University's (CAU), doctoral program. A native Bostonian from birth, Lorenzo had always longed for the experience of attending a Historically Black College and University (HBCU).

In 1997, he met Claudia Lang. They were both business associates and professional colleagues of Dr. Lavell Wilson, President of LPL Consulting Corporation, who had recently passed away. They met at a meeting requested by Dr. Wilson's widow, Patricia, who was meeting with all the Corporation's business associates. After years of professional friendship and camaraderie, Lorenzo Jr. proposed to Claudia while attending the Atlanta Fernbank Museum of Natural History Valentine's Day Dance on Saturday, February 14, 2004. They exchanged marriage vows at the Jimmy Carter Presidential Library and Museum in Atlanta on June 18, 2005. Lorenzo's sons, Derek and Jared, his aunt Lorene, and his father, Lorenzo Pitts, Sr., were a part of the wedding party. Claudia's daughters, Lisa, Paula, Mona, her father, Reverend Claude Lang, brother Reverend John E. Lang, sisters Nancy, Gloria, Phyllis, Hazel, son-in-law Robert, grandchildren Jonathon, Claudia, Claude, Lawrence, Nieces Zaria, Jaila, and close friend Annette De Lavallade, and other immediate family members and close friends also participated in the wedding ceremony. Other close family members and friends from Boston, Indiana, Illinois, New York, New Jersey, Washington, D.C., Louisiana, Texas, and Georgia (Greater Atlanta Metropolitan Area) attended and/or participated in the wedding, reception, and other weekend festivities. This was the first gathering of Lorenzo's and Claudia's families and friends.

On December 12, 2005, Lorenzo Jr. completed his studies and dissertation, *"The Impact of Student Outcomes, Attrition, and Persistence of Integrating Technology Into Teaching and Learning: Implications for Administrative Instructional Change."* This conferred upon him the Doctor of Education (EdD) - Educational Leadership degree. Lorenzo participated in the commencement ceremonies in May of 2006, and his father, his longtime companion Pechola, and Claudia joined other proud parents and spouses on the grounds of the CAU campus for the graduation ceremonies and celebrations. Dr. Charles R. Stith from Harvard University, former Ambassador to Tanzania and civic leader in Boston's inner-city neighborhoods, was the guest commencement speaker.

Overjoyed about Lorenzo Jr. receiving his Doctorate, Lorenzo Sr. was elated to find that Ambassador Stith, a fellow Bostonian and business acquaintance, was the commencement speaker.

What a wonderful celebratory weekend. He was happy and knew that Helen would be proud if she could have joined him and their son to celebrate this extraordinary family achievement.

Death of Reverend Claude Lang

Reminiscences of Lorenzo Pitts, Jr. on Past Events

March 2009 was a difficult month. My wife, Claudia, had spent several weeks in Northwest Indiana and the Chicago area with her family. The family members had been summoned to the hospital bedside of her father, Evangelist Reverend Claude Lang. Reverend Lang was an ordained minister and a respected and well-known community member for eighty years. He was a wise man, the Patriarch to 138 family members (six children and numerous grand- and great-grandchildren) across the country, who looked up to him for spiritual and moral guidance, inspiration, and wisdom.

At one hundred and seven years, he demonstrated the phenomenal ability to embrace and adapt to the adversities and challenges accompanying longevity and living in America as an African-American male. He was born in Langsdale, Mississippi, and raised by his father, Frederick Lang, and grandfather, Smiley Lang, son of Colonel Clement Davenport Lang, owner of Langsdale Plantation, after his mother, Annabelle Lang, died. When his grandmother, Louisa Clog Lang, died, the family became a part of the "Great Migration' from the South to the North, ending up in Northwest Indiana. My son Jared and I had the opportunity to visit the Langsdale Plantation during our road trip in 2019.

He was married to Claudia's mother, Hazel Watson Lang, Church Pianist and Scribe for 60 years. Two years after her death, at the age of 92, he married his second wife, widowed Missionary Sara Magee, who passed seven months into the marriage after undergoing a heart operation. At age 96, he married his third wife, widow Ida Lacefield of East Moline, Illinois, an accomplished accordion musician and cake designer. The vintage couple enjoyed a blissful and loving marriage for nine years filled with many wonderful family vacations, including the Lang Family Pilgrimage to the Lang Plantation in Langsdale, Mississippi, religious services, social engagements, and community and family events. As Claudia's stepmother (soon to become my stepmother-in-law), we were glad she could attend and participate in the wedding celebration. She passed away on November 15, 2005, from Heart Disease.

Reverend Lang was known as Big Daddy to the grand and great-grandchildren and Dad Lang to church members who looked up to him as their spiritual leader and confidant. He was 104 years young, full of zest, when he traveled to Atlanta to walk Claudia down the aisle at our wedding at The President Jimmy Carter Presidential Library Chapel. It was the most beautiful sight to behold. Dad Lang passed away peacefully on March 11, 2009, at home, after sharing one last message to family members about God's salvation. I flew from Boston to the Chicago – Northwest Indiana area to join Claudia and the Lang family to celebrate his life and participate in the "Homegoing Services" for my beloved father-in-law, with whom I enjoyed his visits to Atlanta, many hours of birthday and family celebrations, and garnering words of wisdom from our conversations.

"With long life will I satisfy Him and shew Him my salvation"
Psalms 91:16

Death of Lorenzo Pitts

SR: REMINISCENCES OF LORENZO PITTS, JR. ON PAST EVENTS

Several days after the services and final details for Dad Lang were completed, I returned to Atlanta with Claudia. Shortly thereafter, I received a phone call informing me that my dad had been taken to the Emergency Room. We knew that he was ill, but we did not know how sick. I immediately returned to Massachusetts, taking the first flight to Boston.

After visiting Dad in the hospital and talking to the doctors, I started learning medical terminology that comes from the Lung Cancer TNM staging system. TNM stands for Tumor, Node, Metastasis. Thymus Cancer: Range I to IV. Stage I Survival Rate - 96%. Stage II- 86%. Stage III- 69%. Stage IV- 50%. The higher the stage, the lower the survival rate and life expectancy. In Dad's case, he had stage IV and a life expectancy prognosis of six months, which means the tumor invasion was malignant and had metastasized. And the survival rate meant the chances of surviving five years were less than 5% compared with stage I, in which the survival rate would be 96%. We were in a situation where the doctors explained that his tumor could have come from various sources. It could have come from his occupation, could have come from lifestyle, or it could have come from toxin exposure.

During World War II, Dad was in the Navy, and the Navy ships built before 1980 were known for asbestos-related maladies. Also, his career was painting, paper-hanging, and small construction projects; therefore, he often dealt with chemicals. He mixed his paints, but he was never a smoker. The cancer he had was called Thymus Carcinoma, a rare and aggressive type of cancer. The tumor was in a place in his body that produces the white blood cells that fight infection. So, that part of the body makes things that keep him sick. And in the way that it manifests itself to him, the cough was actually a result of his right and left lungs filling with liquid, so there was less and less volume to breathe. That is why he got a cough. The cancer was so rare that they could not enter his name in the Cancer Research database because his name could not be shielded. Research indicates that there are 1 to 1.5 cases per million people annually.

From the first of April through the late summer, Dad was back and forth in the hospital every 30 to 45 days. The hospital would not let him go home. They would always release him to a different rehab center. Dad passed on September 3, while he was in the rehab center in West Roxbury, surrounded by family members.

Lorenzo Pitts, Sr. had survived the Jim-Crow racist south, and sharecropping. He had witnessed the lynching of a fellow Black male and endured the adversities of racism and Jim Crow laws. He served as a U.S. Navy Steward on a Destroyer Escort ship during World War II. Ultimately, he endured the loss of the love of his life, Helen, the mother of his two oldest sons, in 1948, and the death of his second wife, Rosalee, the mother of ten of his children, in 2005. Lorenzo Pitts, Sr., was a loving and dependable son, brother, spouse, father, and accomplished businessman and entrepreneur. He was a patriarch: a father, grandfather, great-grandfather, a community and civic leader, and one of the few African-American millionaires in Roxbury. He was a tenacious worker, a humanitarian, and was revered by his peers and community. It is thought that his last moments of clarity and acceptance that God might call him home at any moment brought forth memories of his life, some glorious, some uncomfortable, and many sentimental…from Texas to Boston, from sharecropper to a multi-millionaire.

Family Turmoil

The 12 heirs of my father, the Patriarch, proved to be a challenge for the sole person designated as trustee, me, his oldest son. When he passed away, I was notified by the estate attorney and my half-sister that there were provisions in the will as well as the estate plans that they could not disclose to me until Dad had passed. I was later informed that there were two additional executors, so now his will revealed three instead of one. I was unaware of this; however, I discovered that he signed it one week before he went to the Emergency Room on March 27th. The document had been prepared while I was away attending my father-in-law's funeral. The legal term for the document is called a codicil, which was the first codicil; you can make different changes to wills, then number the changes. That one change was the first codicil. The codicil named my half-sister, Willetta Givens-Pitts, and her attorney, Terry Mond, the estate attorney, as executors of the will and Estate Plan, which meant there were three designated executors to carry out my Dad's wishes and Estate Plan.

My father's business was Lorenzo Pitts, Inc. (LPI). Within the business, we had a property management firm. We had vehicles and 14 to 16 employees at his death. After his passing, the most significant stressor was figuring out how the business functioned, the operations, how to meet the basic needs, payroll, and vendor payments. On top of that, we still had to get my father, the Patriarch, buried in his final resting place. This was a significant and pressing problem. We needed ten thousand dollars in cash for his burial, and we would not be appointed as executors by the probate court until after October 21st. That was the date that we received his death certificate. We could not distribute funds, have access to funds, or sign checks until we were officially appointed executors by the probate court. That meant that we had to borrow money from one of my other half-sisters to bury him. It also came to our attention that he did leave cash in his apartment in the metal strongbox. The cash immediately became part of his estate upon his death. However, Willetta Pitts-Givens, my half-sister, took the money and told us there was none to distribute. She took the cash but left the wrappers that told you how much was inside the wrapper, which was her way of being "Willetta," her usual self.

Needless to say, the disagreements between Willetta and her siblings, including me, when our father was involved with the business's operations, resurfaced after both parents died. During their Probate Court depositions, many of them spoke of ill feelings toward one another, a toxic and sometimes violent home environment that they grew up in. After their mother, Rosalee, died in 2005, my father tried to 'heal old wounds' by helping his children financially, when possible, and holding a family Christmas holiday gathering and dinner for them and their spouses in hopes that family relationships would improve. Several such gatherings took place in 2006, 2007, and 2008. One of the children in their court deposition stated, "...my mother said before she died on her deathbed that he and my mother had a conversation the day before she died, and he said this is the last time that he's going to say it, that my mother asked him to forgive her for what she did and the pain that she had caused. It was both of them, and for the kids not to carry her pain against him."

Tensions mounted concerning the funeral arrangements. We disagreed on everything from his burial attire to the will. My sister suggested that he wear an outfit that reminded her of a summer event she held called "White Night," where everyone would dress up in white clothes, and he wore a white suit. I disagreed because the people who knew him understood he was a proud businessman and spent most of his time in business attire. I, along with the other brothers and sisters, thought it inappropriate to bury him in something that was not his typical business attire. This caused friction because Willetta found out through the funeral director that if she was not the eldest child, and our father was not married, then the true eldest child had the final say-so of what would be done at the funeral. This did not sit well with Willetta. We originally planned to have the viewing before the funeral. However, we soon realized it was insufficient for the neighborhood and the community to participate.

Our family business was property management. It consisted of many buildings and apartments for more than 1,000 people. Additionally, there were agreements with the vendors, contractors, politicians, and friends Dad associated with throughout the years. Dad made Boston his permanent residence in 1950 and lived there until his death in 2009. So, he had been in business for 59 years. After consideration, it was decided without consensus (Willetta being the dissenting sibling) that we should have two viewings for Dad. One viewing would occur on Friday evening, with the main viewing on Saturday before the funeral services. We were presented with a proclamation from the City Council of Boston in recognition of his contributions to the city and the affordable housing community, and his involvement in community and civic affairs for nearly 59 years. Thanks to the funeral directors, everything went well, including the repast and the welcoming of Dad's family members from Texas and California. Our father, a World War II veteran, was funeralized and buried in his business attire in the veteran's section at the Massachusetts National Cemetery on Saturday, September 13, 2009.

I regret that I was unable to fulfill all of my father's burial wishes.

"I will ask you, Sonny. Please, I hope it will not be too much for you. I hope I'm not asking for too much. I trust and hope, within all my heart, that you and Robert will find the time and understand how important this means to me. I'm asking you now, please, please, bury me next to Helen in the grave wherever is near her. If possible, let my casket touch her casket. I know somewhere we will meet again and hold hands and laugh and talk. This is a, perhaps, too much for me to ask, but at this moment, at this time in my life, I am not thinking about if it's too much now."

8

MANAGING THE ESTATE

After we completed Father's burial, everything went to hell once it was disclosed that the business was going to be passed to his heirs. If everyone had cooperated, settling his estate would have been easy. However, not everyone decided to collaborate. Willetta and the estate attorney chose not to cooperate. They (Willetta Heir/Executor and the Estate Attorney / Executor) agreed to collaborate to oppose our father's will and wishes in the estate documents. The Estate Attorney's lack of knowledge regarding the business's operations and complexities made conversations challenging, and cooperation impossible. However, I was committed to following my Dad's wishes.

A few rules of business were written back in the 80s. However, the oldest rule was established in 1969. When different government and presidential administrations changed, the rules and federal regulations were either updated or grandfathered. And as different presidential administrations came in and left, the rules were either updated or carried forward. We had two trusts, Esperanza and Fort Hill. Another complication was that we had multiple partnerships: Loscoco Estate, U.S. Housing and Urban Development (HUD),

State of Massachusetts Housing Investment Corps (MHIC), and low-income housing tax credit partner Gardner, Crawford, Thane (GCT). We had business arrangements for the different projects, which consisted of about 300 units of affordable housing. The number of buildings may have been in the neighborhood of about 18 to 20.[15]

My father's company, Lorenzo Pitts Inc. (LPI), was established in 1980 to provide affordable housing in some of Boston's low-income, non-white neighborhoods. At one point, the Corporation held one hundred buildings with over 1,000 housing units. It was a large operation employing one hundred people in the maintenance department alone. Ninety percent of this portfolio was affordable units. This was in the 1980s when Dad's company was one of five companies in various locations, including Boston, which was part of the Demonstration Program, known as "Demo-Dispo."

Demo-Dispo was a test of best practices and proof of concept of what we now call Section 8 Vouchers. There were other Black men in the property development and management business. There were two at the time my father and Cruz started. They mentored three more to enter the property development and management business, so at one point, there were five minority developers in the Boston area. By the time of my father's death in 2009, there were only two left: Lorenzo Pitts, Inc. and Cruz Management Corporation. Today, only Cruz remains a minority-owned entity.

After we received Dad's death certificate on September 21, 2009, we had to address the central issue regarding the estate. The amount of cash flow was insufficient to take care of the ongoing expenses of the projects, which needed rehab and servicing of debt. We owed our vendors $7 million towards long-term debt, which was the government's way of putting previous developers' cost on the back end of a failed project as a poison pill to keep the developer from being able to enter into a buy/sale agreement with anyone unless the government HUD approved, which they never would.

While dealing with the challenges of managing an operation that was not generating enough cash flow, it came to my attention that our estate attorney and my sister decided to defraud the other heirs, not follow my father's wishes, and defraud the estate for their benefit and not for anyone else's. The Estate Attorney / Executor had little or no knowledge of the business's operations and complexities.

From Sharecropper to Multimillionaire

U.S. Department of Housing and Urban Development (HUD)

I was not involved in accounting, compliance-reporting, or compliance-auditing until May 1, 2008, when I relocated to Boston to be with Dad day-to-day. I realized that policies, procedures, and general business practices needed to be updated or implemented to improve our ongoing, future operations and obtain a "clean audit." I commuted between Atlanta and Boston, spending every other weekend in Georgia. I thought that Claudia, with her B.S. in Management and Master of Public Affairs, coupled with her experience serving as CEO and other executive leadership positions, would be an asset to the work that needed to be done (See Claudia's C.V. in Appendix A.).

We worked on updating LPI's job descriptions, personnel handbook, administrative policies, and operating procedures. In Boston, I was available 24/7, ready to handle emergencies, business discussions, family planning, and spending time together. I lived with my dad until an apartment became available in his private, triple-decker apartment building at 691 River Street, Hyde Park. It was a time of reflection: strengthening our father-son bond, sharing his wishes for the family, discussing business operations, watching "The Judge Judy Show" and old western television shows, among other things. We worked as a team, and I was his designated driver. Wherever he went, I went. He introduced me to LPI's business associates, bankers, city, state, and federal administrators. We also met with affordable-housing management operators and other community and civic organization leaders, vendors, and tenants.

One of the things that we had to try to do was to figure out the entanglements, what assets we had, and what assets we could get. The assets were not his alone. This meant we had to figure out how to operate with only the two types of Section 8 subsidies. In the first type, the client-held subsidy stays with the renter. The individual renter deals directly with the landlord to finalize the agreed-upon rental cost; the renter pays 30%, and HUD pays 70%. When the tenant vacates the property, they take that potential subsidy with them, and the landlord sees nothing until another HUD tenant rents the unit.

With our projects, things were different. The clients could come and go, and once you went through the process of certifying the client, you would submit them to HUD, and the client would get approval to receive the subsidies. Dad had shown that going with this "project-based" Section 8 subsidy was better. This meant that the subsidy stayed with the unit, and when renters came and went, the landlord would submit them to HUD for certification, and they would get approval to receive the subsidy. The subsidies would come to the landlord, and the tenant would pay the 30%, and they would be on a lease basis. The leases would be on an annual basis with an annual renewal, in which the tenant had to undergo a recertification process, which meant, by doing their taxes, they had to bring certain documents in each year and go through a process of certifying they are still in the condition they were in, or had their condition changed, in terms of the number of people in the household, and so on."

9

HOW TO STEAL INTERGENERATIONAL WEALTH

- Acquire a Codicil to the Will when the benefactor is in a weakened state, and the benefactor's demise is projected to be near and keep it a secret.
- Submit a Fraudulent Inventory of the Estate's assets to Probate Court.
- Challenge the validity of the Trusts. Probate Court refers the case to Land Court.
- Manage and expend all funds generated from Trusts' assets.
- Set up a new Board of Directors consisting of three people: The original Estate executor, Codicil Co-executor/Heir, and Codicil Co-executor/Estate Attorney.
- Become the personal Attorney to one of the heirs.
- Hold a Board of Directors meeting to terminate the original Estate Executor. Exclude the original Estate Executor from all decisions and operations relating to the Estate of the benefactor. Bar the original Estate Executor from the benefactor's properties and stop their wages and benefits.

- Government facilitation: HUD refusal to recognize beneficiaries as owners of the trust properties and withhold subsidy payments.
- Rockland Trust Bank determines it's not in their best interest to convert the past due balloon notes into mortgages for the Trusts.
- Negotiate with local non-profit development corporations to purchase in majority of the non-Trust portfolio.
- Codicil Co-executors liquidate non-trust portfolio for less than market value.
- Hold distribution of funds from beneficiaries, including educational institutions, charities, etc.

The Story Behind the Story

While dealing with the challenges of managing an operation that was not generating enough cashflow, it came to my attention that our estate attorney and my half-sister had decided that they did not want to follow my father's wishes; they wanted to defraud the other heirs for their own benefit.

Sometime after Dad had passed, I came to find out that Willetta had been illegally writing checks to herself and to the estate attorney, Mond. They were using funds from the two trusts, Esperanza and Fort Hill, which were generating the most cash flow. They did this by transferring funds from the Trust accounts to the Estate account.

Over the course of nearly ten years, Willetta and Mond carried out a series of nefarious steps to defraud my father's other heirs of their rightful inheritance.

The steps happened starting in March of 2009, when my father first learned that he had stage 4 thyroid cancer.

Upon my father's death, I found out there was a Codicil to the Will. It turns out that Willetta and estate attorney Mond had been trying for months, and Dad wouldn't sign it. He finally signed it a week before he went into the ER because Willetta threatened to beat up Pechola, my father's companion of more than 20 years. Pechola was in Boston caring for Dad during his illness. Dad cared for her several years ago when she had pancreatic cancer. He couldn't think of any other way to protect Pechola. Willetta said, "If you sign it, I won't bother her." He signed it a week before I learned that he was in the ER. He had known he was ill for a while. But Dad couldn't protect Pechola because Willetta and several of the other siblings were being absolutely horrible to her. Pechola was so upset that she wanted to leave and go back to New Jersey, but her love for Dad wouldn't let her. The idea was that Dad would sign the Codicil but Attorney Mond insisted that no one could tell me.

The following is the private conversation Attorney Mond had with my Dad regarding adding Willetta and himself as executors to his will through this Codicil. *(Reported in a deposition of Terry Mond*

December 7, 2010; Commonwealth of Massachusetts, The Trial Court, Probate and Family Court Department. Re: Estate of Lorenzo Pitts, Sr.)

Attorney Mond said my Dad said, "Can we put in the documents that you would be the attorney for the estate?"

And Mond's answer to him was, "I've never actually seen anybody do that in an estate planning document. I don't know. It's possible people do that, but I've never seen it. You can put anything you want into an estate planning document. My guess would be that it wouldn't be enforceable because, you know, the "___" whoever the executors were, it would be their choice, you know, who they want to would be their choice, you know, who they want to represent them. And therefore, I don't think it would be enforceable."

And he said, "Well, is there any other way I can ensure that you would still be there to help with this?"

And I said, "The only other way that I know you could do that would be to install me as a coexecutor." End of deposition.

Dad died in September, less than six months after the Codicil was signed.

As the Estate's Attorney, and Co-executor, Attorney Mond now had the power and authority to manage and run the entire Estate of Lorenzo Pitts, Sr. as he wished, for his and Willetta's personal financial benefit and gain. Willetta now had the power and authority she always desired with Mond, her personal Attorney, on her side.

In the first probate hearing in October 2009, the Codicil was entered, and Willetta Pitts (CFO), Lorenzo Pitts, Jr. (COO), and Terry Mond, Estate Attorney, were officially recognized as trustees and co-executors.

My half-brothers and sisters objected to our father's Will. They claim the reason they were bringing the objection was because they claimed my dad wasn't in his right mind and that I, being the original executor and eldest son, had an undue influence over him, to the detriment of the other heirs. It was in December 2009 that they sought to nullify Lorenzo Sr.'s Will.

We ended up in a situation where Mond got my half-brothers

and sisters together and said, "If you support me and Willetta when we go to court, each one of you will get $1 million by December, 2009." If they had truly understood the situation, they would have known that would not happen, but my half-siblings bought into it, and we went to probate court. All of the respondents and the Co-Executors were required to give depositions. The individual depositions are shown in court filings. The children's depositions provided the estate attorney with enough information about the family and the siblings' interrelationships to see their individual weaknesses, strengths, and the personal role each played in the family. It is my belief that the depositions enabled Attorney Mond to assess and use the family's weakness to the advantage and benefit of himself and Willetta.

Throughout this time, we managed to hold off all the different agencies and banks. HUD, BHA, MHIC, Gardner, Crawford & Thane – Tax Credit Project, Rockland Trust (Holder of balloon Notes), etc., and kept the projects running. We got HUD to put in place a process in which they continued to pay the Housing Assistance Subsidy (HAP) subsidies 70/30, as if my dad were still alive. While affairs were still in probate court, they could do that. Attorney Mond made sure that happened because that was in his best interest, as he could siphon off funds from it.

The next step of their plan involved Willetta and Attorney Mond submitting to the Probate Court a fraudulent Inventory of the Estate's assets, listing the properties of Esperanza Trust and the Fort Hill Trust as part of my father's personal property. This happened in December of 2009, thus enabling him and Willetta to continue to control the properties and its assets, which they did. The probate judge then referred the case to Land Court to determine if the Trusts were valid. Mond claimed that the trusts had terminated due to the 'Concept of Merger,' derived from a 15th-century English law. Massachusetts, as one of only a handful of U.S. Commonwealth states, maintains some laws with those origins. It was fraudulent to claim that the 'Doctrine of Merger' meant that the trusts terminated upon the death of my father. Mond insisted that the trusts were part of Dad's personal assets when he passed, and therefore, they would not pass free of probate. This was another underhanded action taken to steal our inheritance.

Throughout 2010, we went through each of the supervisory agencies to facilitate the transfer of ownership to the heirs and to see if my father's heirs could be recognized as owners under HUD's regulations. HUD could take or seize the inventory of 300 affordable housing units without compensation to the heirs, then HUD would get the benefit from them instead of the family. We were able to successfully fight off all of those efforts.

However, in January, 2011, Willetta and Mond decided that restructuring was too much of a problem. They opted for liquidation of the enterprise, easier, over and done! They eliminated me through illegal maneuvers so that I would not have any executive responsibility or authority, rather than continuation of the enterprise. To accomplish this, they created a three-person board consisting of the two Codicil Co-Executors Willetta Pitts, heir and Estate Attorney Mond, and myself, the original Estate Executor, and proceeded to call a board meeting. By this point, I had returned to my residence in Atlanta to work on Estate, Trust, and Title matters from there. As I was absent from Boston when the meeting was called, I asked my brother Robert to attend the board meeting as my representative, as he was the other heir to the trusts. Willetta and Mond refused to allow this. They positioned a private security guard to prevent Robert from entering the building for this one and only meeting of the board. Willetta and Mond were the only people present at that board meeting, and the only item on the agenda was a motion to terminate me as the third board member and my position. *See Appendices.* This sneaky action was an additional step taken in the process of stealing our inheritance.

From this point on, I was excluded from all decisions and operations relating to the Estate of Lorenzo Pitts, Sr. The company's van was immobilized with a tire clamp (sometimes called a Denver boot), my health and life insurance were canceled, I was barred from LPI's office, and my wages were stopped. I was locked out of my father's personal apartment building at 691 River Street, and my personal belongings were removed. I didn't have a job or a place to stay in Boston. None of the family members, including myself, Robert, or my half-siblings, received communications from or had access to information about the operations and management of our father's Estate, with the sole exception of Willetta. From this point on, everything was handled by her, with Mond's assistance. After this underhanded action, I returned to Georgia to assess the situation and determine next steps.

As head of the family's business enterprise, with the estate lawyer on her side to advise, Willetta now had what she had always wanted. Mond was not only the estate lawyer, but he was also Willetta's personal Attorney. My father had told me he didn't want anyone other than his heirs to be part of the LPI company, so Mond's involvement was directly against Dad's wishes. However, Mond reported to the judge that my father had told him differently. Both Mond and the judge were white, so the situation, to me, bore the stench of 'White Privilege' as the judge overlooked what the family had to say.

In December of 2009, I began to suspect that Attorney Mond and Willetta were doing things that were not in the best interest of the Estate. I began researching court cases involving the doctrine of merger in Massachusetts. It became clear to me that we were the rightful beneficiaries, and the Trust should be passed to Robert and me, free of probate. I realized that it was time to get a lawyer. In March 2011, we hired attorney Gregory Aceto of Aceto, Bonner, and Prager, PC, of Boston, MA, as our primary attorney for the Trusts. He advised me that if I were to decide to sue my father's Estate, it would be wise to resign as co-executor. I resigned shortly thereafter.

Probate Court handles matters of inheritance, but since much of this inheritance was tied up in real estate, the Massachusetts Probate Court referred our case to the Land Court to determine whether the Trusts were valid and who were the rightful heirs of the Trusts. So, Robert's and my ownership, as the original heirs to the trust, would be challenged in the Land Court.

The Land Court's process dragged on from 2011 to 2015. Trusts that should have been passed on to us 'free of probate' ended up in a gruesome, expensive, and lengthy court battle. The entire process was "slow-walked." There were countless court delays and no reports forthcoming on the financial and operational status of the trusts. So, Robert and I had to be the 'moving' party, initiating all steps in the case.

It was during these months that I learned that Willetta was illegally writing checks to herself and to the estate attorney, Mond, from the two trusts, Esperanza and Fort Hill, which were generating the most cash flow. This period of unaccountability became another step taken in the theft of our inheritance.

Our case took almost 4 years in the Land Court. There were a number of factors that were used to delay and extend these proceedings. There were requirements from the occasional court dates to provide first accounting, second accounting, and third accounting, etc. We never received any official documentation from the estate attorney in a timely manner. When we finally received the report, it was late and incomplete. When court dates were set, Estate Attorney Mond didn't bother to show up. What we were trying to do was to get a final accounting and to find out the status of the assets. These delays, the "slow-walk," were just another step in the process to steal our inheritance.

On January 9, 2015, the Land Court judge handed down a ruling against my brother and me. The ruling was a surprise!

It was the first time in Massachusetts' history that a case of merger had been found. The case actually became quite famous because it set a legal precedent. During this period, profits were being stripped from the trusts and misappropriated. No financial records or accounting statements regarding the profits were ever reported to the Probate Court, Land Court, or to the beneficiaries.

JUDGEMENT: "This case, commenced in this court April 29, 2011, came on to be tried to the court (Piper, J.). In a decision of even date, the court has made findings of fact and rulings of law. In accordance with the court's decision… issued today,…(January 9, 2015) it is

ORDERED, ADJUDGED, and DECLARED that,

pursuant to the declaration of trust for the Esperanza Trust, dated February 13, 1980, and recorded with the Suffolk Registry of Deeds in Book 9385, Page 247, the trust, if not earlier terminated, terminated upon the death of the settlor, Lorenzo Pitts, Sr., on September 3, 2009, at which time the title to the real estate held in the trust passed, free of any trust, to Lorenzo Pitts, Sr.'s heirs and devisees, as set out in his last will and testament as by codicil last amended prior to his death. Defendants Lorenzo Pitts, Jr. and Robert Pitts took no title to the real estate which constituted the corpus of the Esperanza Trust under its terms at the time Lorenzo Pitts, Sr. died.....

ORDERED, ADJUDGED, and DECLARED that, pursuant to the declaration of trust for the Fort Hill Trust, dated December 1, 1984, and recorded with the Suffolk Registry of Deeds in Book 11658, Page 152, the trust, if not earlier terminated, terminated upon the death of the settlor, Lorenzo Pitts, Sr., on September 3, 2009, at which time the title to the real estate held in the trust passed, free of any trust, to Lorenzo Pitts, Sr.'s heirs and devisees, as set out in his last will and testament as by codicil last amended prior to his death. Defendants Lorenzo Pitts, Jr. and Robert Pitts took no title to the real estate which constituted the corpus of the Fort Hill Trust under its terms at the time Lorenzo Pitts, Sr. died. It is further

ORDERED, ADJUDGED, and DECLARED that the Esperanza Trust terminated pursuant to the doctrine of merger on June 11, 1997, and was not at any time thereafter revived, re-instituted or re-created. From that date forward, the title to the real estate held in the trust was held by Lorenzo Pitts, Sr. free of any trust, and free of any right, title or interest of the defendants. It is further

ORDERED, ADJUDGED, and DECLARED that the Fort Hill Trust terminated pursuant to the doctrine of merger on April 26, 2005, and was not at any time thereafter revived, re-instituted or re-created. From that date forward, the title to the real estate held in the trust was held by Lorenzo Pitts, Sr., free of any trust, and free of any right, title, or interest of the defendants.

It is further ORDERED that today's decision and this judgment dispose of this case in its entirety.

No costs, fees, damages, or other amounts are awarded to any party."[16]

The appeals process began shortly after the Land Court's ruling on January 9, 2015.

"RULING: In May of 2017, the Court of Appeals found that the trusts were valid and that the named heirs were the rightful legatees. "In the case of Mond v. Pitts (Mass. App. Ct. 15-P-686, Aug. 19, 2016), the Massachusetts Appeals Court corrected an erroneous decision involving two trusts created by Lorenzo Pitts, Sr., who passed away in 2009. ... The trusts provided that at his death, "the beneficiaries shall be Lorenzo Pitts, Jr. and Robert Pitts, in equal shares."[17]

The case was remanded to the trial judge to issue the rescript. Months passed. No action was taken. No rescript was issued. Eventually, the heirs brought action against that judge and his superiors for "dereliction of duty."

Finally, we were successful in getting our inheritance returned, including titles and control of both Fort Hill and Esperanza Trusts, which included 82 of the 300 units held in my father's portfolio: Trust and non-Trust properties.

In September of 2017, we started the process of trying to manage the trust properties to carry them into the future as Dad would have wished. We set up an office in Boston near Dudley Square, operating under Cambridge Holdings of Sandy Springs, LLC. (CHSS). Working along with several professional support staff in this office, we had one of my sons, Jared and Robert, and two of his children, daughter Lecia Pitts McLean and Robert L. Pitts (known as Bobby). CHSS' business office was equipped with all the necessary office equipment and furniture. The Trusts' client files from LPI's office were secured, set up, and properly protected in locked files in our business office near Dudley Square in Roxbury, renamed Nubia Square on December 19, 2019.

Bank accounts were established after we received a certified check from the Trust's accounts receivable for each Trust. We received no financial records from LPI office. We soon found out that there were outstanding payables to vendors. We then immediately started paying past-due invoices and making the necessary arrangements to transfer accounts to CHSS.

Throughout these processes, Robert and I were trying to fulfill Dad's wishes: Keeping the properties' ownership in the family, training the next generation to operate and manage the business, and providing affordable housing to families in the Roxbury community. At this point, we were ready to begin our next saga.

United States Housing and Urban Development (HUD) is an organization that is not known as easy to deal with. It is highly bureaucratic and racist in its concepts and policies. HUD's ruling indicated that my brother and I were not qualified to be owners of any property but rather that HUD had a say over the subsidies. Because of the HUD rules, there was an exception to that because my father's Fort Hill and Esperanza properties were trusts. As trusts, they were exempt from this rule from HUD. However, HUD would not recognize this exception and informed us that no subsidies would be coming directly to us. HUD bureaucracy made a decision to not follow their own rules and regulations, and the beneficiaries were not recognized as owners of trust properties.

We were required to hire an intermediary management firm that HUD had approved. HUD would pay the subsidies to the intermediary management firm, and we could then have a contract with the intermediary. The wording of the Trust required the Trust to terminate once the new heirs filed new documents. At the recommendation of our own personal Attorney, we had followed the ruling of the Appellate Court of Massachusetts, and had terminated both Fort Hill and Esperanza Trusts upon my Dad's death. The new Trusts were Fort Hill Trust II and Esperanza Trust II.

There were two parts of the Lorenzo Pitts, Sr. Trusts: the living part of both Trusts in which he received the benefits of the Trusts as long as he was alive; and upon his death the Trusts terminate, and the heir(s) receive the benefits of the trusts. The HUD ruling referred back to 1980 and 1984 when the agency had initially signed with Lorenzo Pitts, Sr. Now, they needed his signature in order to be recognized. Since he had died some six years earlier, that was going to be a bit of a problem. What HUD's representative requested was absurd. and they knew it! They pretended not to know my father was deceased and had been so for more than six years. It was impossible to get the requested signature from our deceased father. Their decision was to not recognize us as the new owners. This was governmental facilitation in the theft of our property.

We set up a Property Management Agreement (PMA) with Cruz Management Corporation (Cruz), a construction, development, and management firm. Cruz is the last remaining development and property management company of the original five minority companies started in Boston in the 1950s through the 1990s.

Through a process lasting over six months, Cruz received the past-due-subsidies, ran the operations of the trusts' properties, and recertified residents on our behalf.

It became apparent that my brother and I would not be able to survive financially. We had little to no authority over our inheritance. The third part of the HUD rule meant that we would not get any benefit from any surplus cashflow until three months after the end of the year. This meant we would run a year from January to December, and then, we could submit a form in April to take benefits of any surplus monies after setting aside reserved funds approved by HUD. The surplus Rule was not hard and fast, but there was an understanding of what was done; A certain percentage that was put in. That percentage was not a part of the written rule, it was just an understanding that the Boston office had.

At the same time, the HUD Boston office lost its designation as the regional management. In 2017, the office was downgraded to a satellite office of the New York region. The New York region is the largest HUD region in the country, and the Boston office basically became a shell operation, and the management was moved to New York City. This was a recipe for even longer wait times.

We, the new owners and heirs of the trusts, never received a single subsidy from HUD. The only company that received subsidies was Cruz, our interim property management company. They were already on HUD's approved list. After HUD finally approved our contract with Cruz, they were able to receive the subsidies on our behalf. Sometime around January, 2018, we were able to make up the accounts payable that were in arrears. We were finally up-to-date. What we had looming in the background or in the room, however, were two elephants.... the two banknotes.

In 2004 and 2005, my father had taken out two balloon banknotes: $1,000,000 for Esperanza Trust and $1,200,000 for Ford Hill Trust, each for five years. In September, 2009, he passed away. In December of 2009, I received a call from the Rockland Trust Bank. They informed me that, even though a hefty interest rate was being paid on the notes each month, the bank was calling in the two balloon notes because they were overdue. What my dad had done with his controller was to list them on the books as a mortgage. They were not mortgages; they were balloon notes. And so, during my mathematical analysis, I had looked at them as being subject to payment sometime in the future, as long as we were paying our monthly interest. I learned that was not the case, and the bank decided that it was in their best interest to force us into foreclosure.

As HUD did not recognize us as the owners and Rockland Trust refused to consider turning the notes into loans and calling in the loans, CHSS would not be receiving HUD subsidies directly for the tenants. The heirs would be shut out of the day-to-day management of the properties as Dad wished. We had no options left for saving and managing the properties, as our father had wished. Time was not on our side. HUD had total control over the tenant subsidies. There was an imminent threat of forced foreclosure by Rockland Trust Bank to collect the face value plus fees on the balloon notes. HUD and Rockland Trust Bank had boxed us into a corner. The properties were at risk of slipping away, in spite of the fact that we had an established management office in Dorchester, in the Dudley Square area, with professional staff to operate and manage the properties. The challenges of securing and holding intergenerational wealth were extremely difficult, and the door was closing on the possibility of our success.

To realize the maximum benefits of the assets for my brother and myself, we hired a real estate agent to see if we could market Esperanza and keep Fort Hill. We came to find out they were worth more together than separately. Certain Boston firms had been identified, which would be able to acquire our properties for about thirty-three cents on the dollar. It would be in our best interest to unload our assets to an entity other than one of these firms. We were able to sell the properties, located in the historic district, to a Washington State operation eager to have a presence in Boston and willing to continue operating them as affordable housing." With much regret, we sold the Esperanza Trust II and Fort Hill Trust II properties, but at a fair market price.

Dad wanted the properties to remain affordable and available to low-income families. He knew we would have challenges holding on to ownership and operational management of the properties, but if we couldn't manage to retain management, he wanted the trust properties to be the last to be sold.

With much regret, we joined the list of families before us who were unable to complete the transfer of intergenerational wealth, the highest percent of them being African-American families.

Along with the two trusts, there were non-trust properties that formed part of my father's Estate. The non-trust portfolio part of the Estate of Lorenzo Pitts, Sr. consisted of one triple-decker building and 218 units of housing in numerous multi-family apartment buildings. Between 2018 and 2020, the two co-executors of the Estate liquidated these buildings – Estate Attorney Mond and Willetta Pitts-Givens, The Lorenzo Pitts, Sr. Estate remains open in Probate Court (May 2025). (See Appendices section for property photos.)

Just like the Trust Properties, the heirs were not provided any information from Mond or Willetta regarding the operational and ongoing status of the Non-trust properties after my dismissal in March 2011. They had been going against the rules and the wishes of the settler, my dad, from the beginning. They really weren't bothered about doing anything else unethical.

I would travel to Boston to visit all the properties, and I actually saw what they were doing. One of the buildings was a part of the Lawrenceville portfolio. The building had been gutted. I found out who was involved, and a cease and desist order was sent to them. We couldn't take one of the buildings in the non-trust portfolio and sell it without selling the other together with it. However, later, the buildings were sold as a package, and Mond and Willetta kept the funds. No information or reports regarding the transactions were ever sent to the heirs. This was a continuation of their illegal and unethical practices.

We found out that my father's private property, the triple-decker at 691 River Street, was listed for sale in the newspaper. We made an investigation, and the newspaper ad did not appear again. However, that property was later sold to an unknown purchaser. Public sources indicate the building: a 5712 sq. ft. multi-family (5+ units) building, with a total of 6 beds, 6 baths, located at 691 River St., Boston, sold for $935,000.00 on February 27, 2018 (MLS# 72259645). The heirs never received any details or reports regarding the sale, financial transaction, or distributions of profits for this building.

We found out about the bulk of the non-trust estate property sales through articles in organizational newsletters and local newspapers. The Jamaica Plains Neighborhood Development Corporation and other entities were beneficiaries of the sales. We also learned that the city of Boston pitched in about $7.5 million. No information or reports regarding Jamaica Plains purchases and transactions were ever sent to the heirs. However, a ribbon-cutting ceremony and celebration relating to the acquisition of LPI's Non-Trust Portfolio was held. No members from the Pitts family were present.

Everything basically just shut down. When we finally received some financial reports, we proceeded to hire a forensic accountant. We were trying to get a final accounting report in order to close Probate. They were using the system to delay and not show up for Court. Our Attorney put in an order for Mond to respond. The judge said, "Ok, you have a compel order; it's called a compel." When we finally went to Court everyone was there, but Estate Attorney Mond did not show up. We had a new Judge, and she was surprised that this case had been going on for so long. She wanted to know about the paperwork associated with the trial. The Court's representatives brought up 2 of the 22 boxes of materials. No business was conducted at that time.

We received the Estate's Final Amended Account Report signed by Willetta Pitts, Fiduciary, on July 10, 2023, and Terry Mond, Fiduciary, on August 7, 2023.

The probate remains open. Distribution to Pitts Family heirs, a $100,000.00 bequest to the United Negro College Fund (UNCF) and a $100,000.00 bequest to Roxbury Community College remain unpaid as of this writing.

"Nothing is settled until settled right.": Quote attributed to President Abraham Lincoln

Summary of Estate Plan and Will

- First, Dad wanted the business to continue. He wanted it to continue in perpetuity. And so, if we couldn't, he did not want to sell the Trust assets.
- The second thing, although there were twelve children in total, eleven of which were still alive, there were two mommies involved.
- Mommy number one, Helen (Heard) Pitts, had two children, myself (Dr. Lorenzo Pitts Jr.) and my brother Robert C. Pitts. I was born on May 19, 1946. My brother was born on March 12, 1948, and my mother passed away three months later on July 3, 1948. (Split Trust Assets 50/50 by designated percentage).

- Mommy number two, Rosalie (Ridgel) Pitts, married my dad when I was four years old and my brother Robert was two years old. She had ten children. (Split Non-Trust Assets by designated percentage.)
- Trusts were created in 1980, the Esperanza Trust, and in 1984, the Fort Hill Trust. Robert and I were the beneficiaries of both trusts.
- Non-Trust Assets (218 Units) to be divided on a Percentage basis

Dr. Lorenzo Pitts, Jr. (25%)
    Willetta Pitts-Givens (25%)
    Ten (10) Remaining Siblings (5%) each

10

MY DAD - PATRIARCH LORENZO PITTS, SR.

Dr. Lorenzo Pitts, Jr.: Escaping the Jim Crow South and becoming a successful entrepreneur and businessperson in the North would be a challenge from the beginning and look impossible for someone observing the process. The Southern system of keeping the Black person down had centuries of customs, local, State, and Federal government laws, and vast quantities of literature to support the ruling classes' intentions.

In the North what we found was a different animal. My dad arrived in Boston with his two young sons from his first marriage and faced the imminent arrival of his first daughter from his second marriage. From January of 1950 to December 1979 the phase of work begins under the auspices of Lorenzo Pitts Painting and Paper Hanging. From 1980 to his death in 2009 he worked under the auspices of Lorenzo Pitts, Inc.(LPI).

Our Story begins in the winter of 1950 as he arrives in Boston and he starts a business. He found that he could bid on contracts, but he was not allowed to be the contractor. He would be allowed to work for the contractor. As an example, he tells a story about his first time bidding on a job. It was a job for one of the large downtown department stores known as Filene's. The person who was handling the contract explained the system to him. He immediately recognized the systemic inequities. He had a visceral feeling the existence of the old Jim Crow Laws of the South, written and unwritten, to marginalize Black people were very much alive and active in Boston. He did not give up! He had a growing family to care for that depended on him.

One of the things he found was that there was not an established Black business sector in Boston. The city was an extremely expensive place to live. The winters were quite brutal, and the Northern business community and the living community had some of the same beliefs that the Jim Crow South had codified into the Black Codes. He found out that he could work in his profession by offering something that was not readily available off the shelf. He found his niche. He had a knack for chemistry. He was able to blend and mix paint in different colors. He could precisely match any color that the client wanted or thought they might want. Also, from 1950 and during the 1960s, paper-hanging was in vogue in New England and the Boston region.

The Roxbury neighborhood of Boston was where the majority of Black people lived. My father was determined to spend time outside of that community. He could live in the Black community, but he could not earn his living in a Black community because they could not afford his services. His services were more expensive than the average painter and paper hanger, but he delivered a product that people outside of Roxbury, in greater Boston and the suburbs, were willing to pay for. So, he ended up finding a few people with whom he would work, finish the job, and they would refer him to others. He would get many jobs and referrals through word-of-mouth that way.

It wasn't until the 70s that he started to work for people other than those that had private residences. He would take jobs working for people who owned entire buildings in the minority community. Some would call these individuals slum-lords, but these were the days before HUD was heavily involved in the process of ensuring adequate housing. It was mainly private White developers renting to poor minorities in the inner city. He came upon a few people who owned multiple buildings. He would be responsible primarily after the tenant vacated the apartment. He would be responsible for getting the apartment back in good condition for the next tenant, cleaned up and painted so that it would be presentable.

The Big Break came in the '70s and '80s and also the '90s, but mainly the '70s and '80s when the Northern inner cities were really racked by crime, drugs, and a general feeling of despair. He would be a part of a small cadre of people that would be able to survive in that environment by being able to bring in their equipment, do the work, and not have the local gangsters take advantage of them. He would make sure that his crew was looked after, and the local neighbors knew who he was.

The key point of change was when he was doing work for a couple of gentlemen who owned part of a housing-unit complex. This was a complex of townhouses in a Revolutionary War historical section of Boston called Fort Hill. There were two owners; one was Caucasian, and one was Black. The Caucasian partner went downtown and dealt with the city, courts, and the infrastructure, and the Black partner rented the units, kept the buildings in compliance with city codes and regulations, and dealt with the tenants. Unfortunately, the minority owner passed away suddenly, and the remaining White partner found himself unable to manage the on-site activities with the tenants. My dad was already working at the complex and had a reputation with the tenants as an honest person and able to do the work. So, the surviving partner approached my dad with an offer. He said he would offer Dad a 49% share, and he would retain 51% share ownership of the complex, and they would become partners. My dad went away and thought about it. Based on his experience with the Jim Crow South the counteroffer that he came back with was that he would become 51% and the White partner would become 49%. (During the period of sharecropping, the sharecropper would be held 100% responsible for all failures, with little or no power to facilitate any changes or input in financial matters. 51% gave him the power along with the responsibility to make any necessary changes.) The White partner accepted the deal, and the partnership began. There were a variety of different buildings. The townhouse complex was known as Fort Hill, and another apartment complex was called Esperanza. There were several other buildings in this partnership. Along with this was the work he was doing in buildings owned by the people with whom he had contracts.

Boston's housing infrastructure, as far as affordable housing and rent control, was separate. There is the traditional Criminal Court, but there is also a Housing Court. There is also a City of Boston agency that handles people who cannot afford to pay a lot for rent. The public/private split was always there. Developers would come in at the city's request and bid on certain buildings and projects. The developers would then rehab the buildings, bring them up to code, and get the certificate of occupancy. The buildings could then be occupied. The problems came when the rents were kept artificially low because of the politicians, the upkeep, the inner-city location of the buildings, how the people were treated, and what the tenants could afford to pay. Over time, the problems were magnified. There was always a gap between what it cost to run the project (operation and maintenance of the buildings) and the incoming revenues, especially during the winter months. Under the auspices of the City of Boston's Housing Inspection Department and the City of Boston's Housing Court the buildings may require significant outlays of funds from developers and landlords, especially during winter months when heating the large buildings is a challenge in Boston's bitterly cold weather and high energy costs.

There were many failures. Developers would fail and walk away from the buildings. At this time, when in the 80's, HUD was more and more involved. There were times when HUD would do certain demonstration projects, hoping to find a system that the political and city structures could both support. What evolved from these trials was the housing voucher system. There are two kinds of vouchers. One for the resident in which the tenant gets the voucher and negotiates with the landlord, and there is a 30% and 70% split. For every 30 cents on the dollar, the tenant would pay, HUD would pay 70 cents on the dollar. The result of this was that 100% of the subsidy Housing Assistance Payment (HAP} would go directly to the landlord.

My dad was involved in the innovative project known as "Demo Dispo," This project flipped the switch. The voucher did not go with the tenant; it stayed with the apartment and the landlord. So, the idea is that this process for qualifying is based on the prevailing Federal and State regulations and eligibility criteria and what the tenant had to be able to do because the rents would be below the Fair Market Rent (FMR). The landlord and the property manager would be responsible for interviewing the tenant and the family and submitting them to HUD for approval for one of these subsidized units. My dad was able to do this quite successfully.

Another thing my dad was able to do that really started him on his way was this: The Housing Court had an enforcement department called the Housing Inspection Department. That Inspection Department had the power to condemn a building if it was deemed unlivable. If a building was condemned, the owner or developer would come to the Housing Court. The judge would be in a situation where it came down to a decision, and the judge would offer the building(s) to other developers in the area, which means that if the developer failed to make the improvements necessary to make the building livable, a manager of last resort would be chosen and the title would be transferred to that manager if they decided to take the buildings. Some of the buildings were so notorious a person could not safely walk in them. The manager had to have their own police details to accompany him into the building.

The local political powers did not want the buildings to be closed and boarded up. But, if the buildings became uninhabitable for decent, safe, sanitary housing and could not meet the sanitary codes, then the judge would go through this process. My dad became the preferred manager of 'last resort.' The Chief Judge of the Housing Court would call him on a Friday morning and tell him if he did not take the job, the plywood would go up, and the people in the building would be put out on the street and would not have a place to stay. He would say, "Okay, Pitts, if you don't take this job, the plywood will go up, and the people in the building will be put out on the street and they won't have any place to stay at all." So, he would take on all these projects that nobody else was willing to do. He built his reputation in that way by taking buildings from the brink to being condemned to a point where they were deemed habitable. There was a group of five minority businesspeople in the Roxbury area that took this process and managed it as a team. That was his cadre of support and his mentoring support system.

My dad was always there for his parents and siblings, paying their way out of sharecropping in Texas in the 1940s, and purchasing a home for them in San Diego, California. He was a caring and responsible husband, and a father who demonstrated stability, strength, generosity, discipline, accountability, and wisdom. He wasn't afraid of work. There always existed mutual respect between him and his tenants, clients, business associates, employees, extended family, and friends. As an African American man born into sharecropping in Texas and a Bostonian for 59 years, he stood tall in his adopted city and among the people of Roxbury. He was a philanthropist and the recipient of numerous awards honoring his contributions to the people of Roxbury and Boston.

By the evening of September 3, 2009, at the glorious age of 85, he had given all he had to his family, friends, Roxbury, and Boston, and quietly slipped away.

I will begin every day by speaking words of Faith and Victory.
I am Blessed. I am Healthy.
I am Prosperous. I am Successful.

Lorenzo Pitts, Sr.

EPILOGUE
WORDS OF LORENZO PITTS, JR.

There are thousands of stories of Estate Attorneys and Estate Executors mishandling Estates, and the heirs' loss of inheritance from the beginning of record-keeping of estate transactions and this is one.

On June 26, the Jamaica Plain Neighborhood Development Corporation (JPNDC) took ownership of 21 multi-family buildings totaling 201 units for $22 million. "This is by far the largest single project we've ever been involved with," said Richard Thai, executive director of JPNDC. (Boston Bulletin, July 26, 2018).

"... but in 2016, about 150 of those units were at risk of being converted to market-rate housing," said Teronda Ellis, CEO of JPNDC, at a ribbon-cutting event Tuesday. Her organization, which works to develop affordable housing across the city, felt that it was important to keep the properties affordable. "It wasn't a question of whether, but of how we do that with our partners," Ellis said. (Bay State Banner, August 26, 2021). Ellis was wrong. It was always the intent of the Pitts family to keep the properties affordable.

What neither JPNDC nor the Pitts family heirs (with the exception of Willetta) knew was that Codicil Co-Executor Willetta and Codicil Co-Executor/Estate Attorney Mond never intended to let the heirs manage and operate the estate. Estate Attorney Mond was also Willetta's personal attorney. Together, they handled every detail of the business operations and made no effort to communicate with other heirs. It was never their intent to allow myself or other heirs to take possession of the properties, business operations, and management. Their mismanagement, and their lack of understanding of the complexities of working with numerous government agencies, institutional biases, and multiple contracts, opened the door to the heirs losing their inheritance.

It was our father's intent that family members own his estate properties, and family members manage and operate the properties and keep them affordable. Helping people live better lives was always extremely important to him. But he also wanted his business to be a family business for the next generation and generations to come.

For decades, he worked tirelessly through the bureaucratic system that governs affordable housing in Boston to provide safe and decent housing to low-income and homeless families. Born into a family of generational Sharecroppers, our father knew the daily struggles and life challenges that low-income families faced every day. As a young man, not quite seventeen, he enlisted in the Navy and entered active duty in Austin, Texas, on February 17, 1942. He served until the end of World War II, with an honorable separation with the rank of Steward Second Class. He used his allotment to buy his family of 10 out of sharecropping and helped them start a new life in San Diego, California. He was an ethical, principled businessperson. He was generous and compassionate, a humanitarian, self-made entrepreneur, a community- and civic-minded long-standing resident of 59 years in Roxbury, and most of all, a man of faith and a family person.

It would have been considerate if JPNDC and other interested parties had done more due diligence and pursued neighborly relations with all of the Pitts heirs before strategizing on how to take over our family properties, our inheritance. All except one of the 12 siblings were born in Boston, all were raised in Boston, and the majority still reside in the city or nearby neighborhoods. There was clearly a misconception that the Pitts heirs planned to convert the properties to market-rate housing. That rumor, that untruth, just fueled the desire for JPNDC and other interested parties to acquire the properties by any means necessary. Our father worked decades and suffered much to provide affordable housing to single mothers, seniors, senior veterans, BHA homeless, and other low-income families, only to have his family disenfranchised and defrauded after his death.

Throughout the years, my other siblings and I have worked with our father in the family business. He loved Roxbury and its people. While he has a legacy of helping disenfranchised people, he also has a legacy of helping his 12 children and their families. He believed the assets of his estate would be the answer after his death for creating intergenerational wealth.

To the best of my knowledge and belief, Dad did not request the Codicil to his Will. But in the last days of his life, prior to his hospitalization for cancer treatment, Willetta and Estate Attorney Mond conspired to obtain his signature in violation of his Estate Attorney Mond's fiduciary responsibilities. At the end of his life, Dad wanted something denied to him in life; he wanted peace and harmony among his children. The Will's assets were never Attorney Mond's and Willetta's to take or to use for their personal benefit, nor was it right for Willetta to have total authority over the entire estate.

Again, ... In the end, it was both the external forces outside the family and the challenges within the family that worked against the transfer of intergenerational Black wealth.

THE ESTATE OF LORENZO PITTS, SR.

Opened

September 3, 2009

Closed

August 7, 2025

ACKNOWLEDGMENTS
FROM S. CLAUDIA LANG PITTS

First, I am thankful and grateful to God for keeping me physically and mentally healthy and sustaining me with the fortitude and passion to manage the tasks necessary for the development, research, writing, and completion of this book. Furthermore, I am thankful for the insight and wisdom He has given to me in putting Lorenzo Sr.'s life story on paper so the generations to come may come to know him and learn.

When I sat down to draft this book in earnest, during the COVID-19 pandemic, I had already started collecting materials and documents for a book about my father, the family patriarch, Reverend Claude Lang. He lived to the impressive age of 107, and his life story is worth sharing and preserving for future generations. He was the patriarch for his 6 children, 37 grandchildren, 65 great-grandchildren, and 27 great-great-grandchildren, and revered by numerous relatives and friends across the country. My father's Homegoing Celebration Services were in March of 2009. We lost Lorenzo's father six months later. After considerable thought, I decided that I should write a book about his father's life story in collaboration with him, and it should be written first.

Thus began the first step in the arduous journey to write this book. As retirees, Lorenzo and I travel often, enjoy the theater and concerts, and spend quality time with family and friends, which often takes precedence over writing. However, what we didn't consider was the extensive amount of time required to deal with the legal issues and court battles related to the closing of his father's will. A journey that began in 2009 continues as of this writing.

Our sincere appreciation goes to my father-in-law, Lorenzo's dad, Lorenzo Pitts, Sr. (deceased 2009), for honoring our request to record his memories of Helen and his early life. Lorenzo, Jr. was only 2 years old, and his brother Robert was less than 4 months old when their mother died. These recordings were instrumental to the development and writing of this book. We can't express our gratitude enough for the hours spent and his tireless efforts to complete this singular task of reflecting on his memories covering more than seventy years. Some of the memories revealed things that were extremely painful and emotionally upsetting to him to relive, and some were heart-wrenching for us to hear. However, it was a joy to hear his voice on the audio recordings, his inflection and quality of delivery sounded as if he was in the room with us. It makes his gift to us even more personal and SPECIAL.

We owe our thanks to Thomas Middleton, Sr. (deceased August 2015), who invited us to vacation with him in August of 2014. We stayed with him at James Island, South Carolina, in his retirement home. Middleton was Pitts, Sr.'s Navy comrade and life-long friend. To Lorenzo Jr. and his brother Robert, Thomas and his wife were known as Uncle Thomas and Aunt Theresa. Theresa was known to have a sweet spirit and a special love for children. Lorenzo, Jr. and Robert had stayed at the Middleton home periodically during their youth whenever his friend needed someone to care for his boys. Life in James Island was easy-going with a laid-back feel. We received a vivacious welcome from day one. During our visit, we couldn't stop talking. We had a conversation after a conversation for days. Uncle Thomas was eager to tell his life story. One day, we suggested, and he agreed to let us record our conversations about his life.

We attended services with him at St. James Presbyterian Church and visited Aunt Theresa's (deceased July 2007) grave in the church's cemetery. Our visit also included brunch at a downtown Charleston restaurant with him and his new lady friend Ercelle Chillis, who had recently retired to James Island. Thomas's face would light up when he spoke of Ercelle. He had a friend. She was highly intelligent, spry, youthful-looking with an infectious smile, and exhibited a zest for life. She had vacationed in Paris, France, the year before with her daughter and son-in-law. During our stay, we had the opportunity to attend one of her 100th Birthday Celebration parties. The outdoor celebration's atmosphere was so jubilant that it was hard to sit still when it was time to eat. Youthful in spirit and heart, Ercelle Moore Chillis passed away on February 22, 2025, at the age of 110. Relatives and Friends came from near and far places to attend her Homegoing Celebration Services at First Baptist Church of James Island on March 8, 2025. Her zest and love for life connected with others and touched their life in an emotional and positive way. We also had a chance to meet Uncle Thomas's granddaughter, who lived nearby and often looked in on him. We all shared lunch at a local restaurant. It was a great, heart-warming, and soul-filling vacation with family. We appreciate Gloria Middleton, Thomas's daughter, for allowing us to use excerpts from his recordings, and providing additional information and clarifying documents, when needed.

I am grateful to my granddaughter, journalist Claudia Owens, who worked hand-in-hand with me in the development, research and the structuring of major parts of the book, taking time and having patience to interview Lorenzo, Jr. for his life's story and our first editing. Her input and work were invaluable and helped to make the production of this book possible.

Perish the thought that I would fail to thank my number one transcriber, friend, fellow AAWWBC member, and author of *"Rain,"* T. Dawn Gatling Coates, for her vitally important contribution to the foundation of this book.

I would like to thank my daughters, Lisa, Paula, and Mona. Throughout our lives together, we have provided support and encouragement to each other's endeavors, with a lot of fun and laughter along the way. I appreciate the support you gave me during your school years as I relentlessly, year after year, pursued my college education, and you became studious students. It was often challenging during the years all of you were away at college at the same time. I was never so proud as on the days each of you received your college degrees. Thank you for your interest and your continued support and encouragement for this project.

A special thanks to my stepsons, Derek and Jared, who were

intent on showing me their father in all his "glory" before we married to be sure I was the "right one" for him, and showing their approval by participating in our wedding ceremony. "No return" gift receipt included! Thank you for helping us with the legal entanglements and real estate matters relating to your grandfather's estate. We are grateful. Lastly, we are proud of both of you and the new business undertaking, "Farm One," the family's first urban vertical farming and Brewing Lab in Brooklyn.

The African-American Women Writers' Book Club (AAWWBC) was organized on February 20, 1995. It has been an integral part of my social and literary education and life. A group of women who loved reading books established the club with the help and support of two Barnes and Noble representatives. The book club is open to the general public, particularly women who live in the vicinity of the Barnes and Noble store in Alpharetta, Georgia, where the monthly meetings convened and continued until the COVID-19 pandemic forced the book club to hold its meetings on Zoom. Along with other AAWWB members, I have enjoyed reading a vast array of literary genres such as mystery, politics, romance, poetry, science, travel, true crime, biographies, self-help, civil rights, current events, fiction, and non-fiction. Our primary focus is the literary works of African-American women writers. However, we also entertain the writings of males and non-Arican-American writers. It has been this wide-ranging reading experience, and the camaraderie with the AAWWBC members that have given me the confidence and encouragement to write my loved one's life stories.

Nothing needs to be said about the Rivergate HOA Book Club. The comradeship, the diversity of literature selected each month, the members' dedication to open communication, and the sharing of their book critiques allowed me to see literature from different perspectives. The experience was empowering and strengthened my resolve to complete this book. Thank you.

I would like to thank my relatives and friends who continuously checked in on my progress and encouraged me to continue my work on the book. Their faith in me that I could complete this time-consuming and arduous job was heart-warming.

I am forever grateful to Frank Eastland of Publish Authority and his team, who guided me through the editing and publishing of *"Soul of Our Family,"* a book of prayers, praises, and poems, a family project with the Lang Watson Foundation, Inc., published in 2021. Again, his support and guidance from the beginning to the completion of this book has been invaluable.

Lastly, special gratitude goes to my loving husband, friend, and co-author for his patience and endurance as we "slow-walked" this book to completion. He contributed oral interviews, recorded memories about his life's experiences, provided source documents, conducted research when necessary, and was always available to answer probing questions and clarify documents, if needed.

APPENDICES

A. Curriculum Vitae of Claudia Lang Pitts
B. Suffolk, SS. Probate and Family Court…In Re: Estate of Lorenzo Pitts
C. Mond/Pitts-Givens – Legal Proceedings
D. Massachusetts Appellate Court decision document
E. Sequence of Legal Events
F. Historical and Family Timeline
G. City of Boston Tribute and Awards
H. Mond/Pitts, Jr. Correspondence
I. Media Articles
J. Suggested Reading List and Suggested Videos
K. Photo Archives

APPENDIX A
CURRICULUM VITAE S CLAUDIA LANG PITTS

S. Claudia Lang Pitts is currently the Founding President & Chief Executive Officer (CEO) for the Lang Watson Foundation, Inc. She is a graduate of St. Joseph Calumet College holding a Bachelor of Science in Management degree, and Indiana University School of Public and Environmental Affairs Master of Public Affairs degree.

She has had an extensive career serving in executive leadership positions as CEO of nonprofit private organizations, business consultant, and a professional grant writer securing millions of dollars for public and private nonprofit entities, and private clients. Her expertise includes work with the private business sector, government, refugee resettlement agencies, and religious organizations.

She spearheaded the Lang Watson Foundation's legacy project "

The Soul of Our Family," published in 2021 by Publish Authority. The book is a collection of prayers, poems and affirmations written by family members across the United States and abroad.

A lover of books and art, Claudia is an active member of two book clubs and enjoys an enriched life as a portrait artist. She resides in Sandy Springs, Georgia with her husband Dr. Lorenzo Pitts, Jr. enjoying the life of retirees.

APPENDIX B

SUFFOLK, SS. PROBATE AND FAMILY COURT
IN RE: ESTATE OF LORENZO PITTS

"In the Court's Order dated November 12, 2010, the Court struck the Affidavit of Objections filed by the Respondents to the extent that it sought to raise an issue of testamentary capacity."

i. The Respondents have failed to state sufficient facts to show that Mr. Pitts made an unnatural disposition of his property.
ii. The Respondents have failed to state sufficient facts to show that Mr. Pitts was susceptible to undue influence.
iii. The Respondents have failed to state sufficient facts to show that Mr. Pitts' estate planning benefited someone who had the opportunity to exercise undue influence.

For information and details about the Estate of Lorenzo Pitts, Sr. Court case: Go to Google search: Mond v. Pitts.

- Lorenzo Pitts, Sr. death on September 3rd, 2009

- Receive death certificate from funeral director. October 2009
- File death certificate in Suffolk County Probate Court, along with Estate Plan and First Codicil to the Will.
- Initial court date: October 2009. Court calendar for Suffolk County Probate Court to probate the will.
- Wait for the judge's appointments of estate executors. After receiving the judge's appointments, they now operate as executors to the will and estate plan, and carry out Lorenzo Pitts, Sr's wishes.
- December: A fraudulent inventory filed. It was filed in order to invalidate the Trusts.
- Suffolk County Massachusetts Probate Judge refers the case to Land Court to determine if the Trusts portions of the estate are valid.
- Suffolk Land Court process lasted from 2011 to 2015 with Lorenzo Pitts, Jr. and Robert C. Pitts becoming the moving party
- Suffolk County Land Court Ruling invalidates both trusts in 2015.
- Appeal is filed with the Massachusetts Appellate Court in 2015.
- Massachusetts Appellate Court ruling reverses Suffolk County Land Court Ruling.
- 2015 Trusts were validated with 2 heirs
- 2017 Lorenzo Pitts, Jr. and Robert C. Pitts take possession of Esperanza Trust and Fort Hill Trust (82 of the estate's 300 units of housing in Boston).

"In the case of *Mond v. Pitts* (Mass. App. Ct. 15-P-686, Aug. 19, 2016), the Massachusetts Appeals Court corrected an erroneous decision involving two trusts created by Lorenzo Pitts, Sr., who passed away in 2009. Lorenzo Sr. created the Esperanza Trust and the Fort Hill Trust, both of which held real estate in Roxbury. While the trusts had a second trustee and at one point, the second trustee also owned 1% of one of the trusts, during his life, Lorenzo Sr. became the sole trustee and sole lifetime beneficiary of both trusts. The trusts provided that at his death, "the beneficiaries shall be Lorenzo Pitts, Jr. and Robert Pitts, in equal shares." The trusts further directed that the trusts would terminate, and that the property be sold and distributed "among the beneficiaries if living."

By Harry S. Margolis
Margolis Bloom and D'Agostino

APPENDIX C

TERRY K. MOND AND WILLETTA PITTS-GIVENS

As They are the Temporary Co-Executors of the Estate of Lorenzo Pitts v. LORENZO PITTS, JR. and ROBERT PITTS.
MISC 11-448148
January 9, 2015
Suffolk, ss.
PIPER, J.
DECISION

I. INTRODUCTION

The temporary co-executors of the estate of Lorenzo Pitts, Sr. (plaintiff or the Estate), Terry K. Mond and Willetta Pitts-Givens, brought this action to have this court determine who holds title to certain properties on Walnut Avenue, in the Roxbury section of Boston (the Esperanza Trust Properties), and on Cedar Street, Hawthorne Street, and Highland Street also in Roxbury (collectively, the Fort Hill Trust Properties). This litigation grew out of disputes among parties, family members of the late Lorenzo Pitts, Sr., about the state of title to this income producing multi-family residential apartment projects at the time of his death. I am called upon to decide whether the title to these properties passed under his will, as the co- executors contend, or pursuant to the terms of the instruments establishing trusts into which the properties titles earlier were placed, as the defendants say.

II. PROCEDURAL HISTORY

On September 24, 2009, prior to the commencement of this action, Lorenzo Pitts, Jr., Willetta Pitts-Givens, and Terry Mond, Esq. petitioned the Suffolk Division of the Probate and Family Court Department of the Trial Court (Probate Court) to probate the last will and testament of Lorenzo Pitts, Sr. The action was opened on the Probate Courts docket at Case No. 09P-2077-EA. Several of Lorenzo Pitts, Sr's other children appeared in the Probate Court to object; they advanced claims of undue influence. On July 19, 2011, the Probate Court issued a memorandum of decision and order granting the Estates motion to dismiss these objections. The Probate Court held there was insufficient evidence to support a finding of undue influence by Lorenzo Pitts, Jr. and Willetta Pitts-Givens upon Lorenzo Pitts, Sr. In the same memorandum, the Probate Court allowed the petition to probate the last will and testament of Lorenzo Pitts, Sr. The Probate Court left to this court the title question now before me, which requires an interpretation of the meaning and effect of the instruments governing the trusts in which title to the Esperanza and Fort Hill Trust Properties stood of record as of the death of Lorenzo Pitts, Sr.

For Additional Procedural History and Court Ruling: See: http://masscases.com/cases/land/2015/2015-11-448148-DECISION.html or Mond v. Pitts 56 N.E. 3d 894

APPENDIX D

APPELLATE COURT OF MASSACHUSETTS

In conclusion, following the death of Lorenzo, Sr., the terms of the Esperanza Trust and the Fort Hill Trust require that each trust terminate upon the recording of a proper certificate pursuant to paragraph 4 of each trust, and distribution thereafter is to be made to Lorenzo, Jr. and Robert pursuant to paragraph 13 of the trusts. The judgment is reversed, and the case is remanded for entry of a new judgment consistent with this memorandum and order.

So, ordered.

Mond v. Pitts 56 N.E. 3d 894

APPENDIX E
SEQUENCE OF LEGAL EVENTS

For information and details about the Estate of Lorenzo Pitts, Sr's. court case, go to Google search: Mond V Pitts.

- Lorenzo Pitts, Sr. death on September 3rd, 2009
- Receive death certificate from funeral director. October 2009
- File death certificate in Suffolk County Probate Court, along with Estate Plan and First Codicil to the Will.
- Initial court date: October 2009. Court calendar for Suffolk County Probate Court to probate the will.
- Wait for the judge's appointments of estate executors. After receiving the judge's appointments, we can now operate as executors to the will and estate plan, and carry out Lorenzo Pitts, Sr's wishes.
- December: A fraudulent inventory filed. It was filed in order to invalidate the Trusts.
- Suffolk County Massachusetts Probate Judge refers the case to Land Court to determine if the Trusts portions of the estate are valid.

- Suffolk Land Court process lasted from 2011 to 2015 with Lorenzo Pitts, Jr. and Robert C. Pitts becoming the moving party
- Suffolk County Land Court Ruling invalidates both trusts in 2015.
- Appeal is filed with the Massachusetts Appellate Court in 2015.
- Massachusetts Appellate Court ruling reverses Suffolk County Land Court Ruling.
- 2015 Trusts were validated with 2 heirs
- 2017 Lorenzo Pitts, Jr. and Robert C. Pitts take possession of Esperanza Trust and Fort Hill Trust (82 of the estate's 300 units of housing in Boston).

"In the case of *Mond v. Pitts* (Mass. App. Ct. 15-P-686, Aug. 19, 2016), the Massachusetts Appeals Court corrected an erroneous decision involving two trusts created by Lorenzo Pitts, Sr., who passed away in 2009. Lorenzo Sr. created the Esperanza Trust and the Fort Hill Trust, both of which held real estate in Roxbury. While the trusts had a second trustee and at one point, the second trustee also owned 1% of one of the trusts, during his life, Lorenzo Sr. became the sole trustee and sole lifetime beneficiary of both trusts. The trusts provided that at his death, "the beneficiaries shall be Lorenzo Pitts, Jr. and Robert Pitts, in equal shares." The trusts further directed that the trusts would terminate, and that the property be sold and distributed "among the beneficiaries if living."

By Harry S. MargolisMargolis Bloom and D'Agostino

APPENDIX F
HISTORICAL AND FAMILY TIMELINE

Timeline

Pitts Family Timeline		Historical Timeline
	1845	11th President James K. Polk Elected
Napoleon Pitts (Enslaved in Mississippi)	1846	
Annie (Ross) Pitts was born	1850	Fugitive Slave Act, September 18th
	1857	Dred Scott Decision
	1861	President Inauguration March 4th
	1861	Mississippi's secession from the United States Union

Civil War 1861 – 1865

	1863	President Lincoln's Emancipation Proclamation
	1863	Assassination of President Lincoln, April 15th
	1863	V. P. Andrew Johnson assumes the Presidency on April 15th
	1865	13th Amendment / Outlaw of Slavery
	1865	General Sherman Field Order Number 15-January
	1865	Start of Black Codes
	1865	Founding of the Ku Klux Klan / Pulaski, TN Dec.24th

Reconstruction Period 1865-1877

	1869	14th Amendment Citizenship of Freed Slaves
	1869	End of President Johnson's Presidency, March 4th
Birth of Albert Pitts, born into Sharecropping, Texas	1870	15th Amendment Right to Vote for Black Men
	1871	Civil Rights Enforcement Act / Protection from Violence
Birth of Mollie Wright, wife of Albert Pitts	1874	
	1875	2nd Civil Rights Act / Public Places (Anti-Discrimination Law)
	1876	End of Congressional Reconstruction

Jim Crow Laws 1877 - 1965

	1881	Booker T. Washington's Tuskegee Industrial Institute
	1891	Separate Jim Crow Coach Law for Trains
	1896	Plessy vs Ferguson (Separate but Equal)
Birth Minnie Lee (Stone), wife of Napoleon Pitts	1898	
Birth of Napoleon Pitts, Sharecropper, Texas	1899	
	1909	Start of the NAACP
	1914	Start of World War I
Birth of Lorenzo Pitts, August 13,	1924	
	1929	Start of the Great Depression
	1930	Sherman, Texas, Riot & Lynching of G Hughes, May 3rd
	1933	32nd President Franklin D. Roosevelt's inauguration on March 4th
	1939	End of the Great Depression

Beginning of World War II, Sept. 7, 1939

	1941	Japan launches a surprise attack on Pearl Harbor on December 7th
	1941	The United States declared war on Japan on December 8th
Lorenzo Pitts enlists in the U.S. Navy	1942	
Pitt's family in San Diego, CA, February 6,	1942	
Served on USS Nitro (AE-2), an ammunition ship, and USS Frances M. Robinson DE-220	1945	U.S. drops Atomic Bombs in Japan on August 6th & 9th (Hiroshima and Nagasaki)
January 24th, Helen Lucille Heard marries Lorenzo Pitts (In El Dorado, Arkansas)	1945	V-E Day (Victory in Europe) End of WWII, May 8th
	1945	V-J Day (Victory over Japan) August 15,
	1945	Official Day for America to recognize the ending of World War II, Sept. 2,
Lorenzo Pitts was honorably discharged from the Navy	1946	

Post-War Period

Birth of Lorenzo Pitts, Jr., Boston on May 19th	1946	
Birth of Robert Charles Pitts on March 12th	1948	
Death of Helen Lucille Heard Pitts, age 23, July 3rd	1948	
Pitt's family in San Diego, CA, February 6, 1945 – July 3, 1948	1948	
Lorenzo Pitts, Sr., marries Roselee Ridgell, December (El Dorado, Arkansas)	1949	
Lorenzo Sr. & Rosalee set up housing in Boston	1950	
Started the business, Painting and Wallpapering Hanging	1950	Start of the Korean War: June 25th
Death of Mollie (Wright) Pitts	1951	
	1953	Armistice July 27th

Civil Rights Era

	1954	Beginning of the Civil Rights Movement
	1954	Brown v. Board of Education of Topeka
	1955	Montgomery Bus Boycott, December
	1955	Lynching of Emmett Till
	1955	The Vietnam War started on November 1st
	1958	NASA launched Explorer I on January 31st
	1961	35th President John Fitzgerald Kennedy
	1963	Assassination of Medgar Evers, Jackson, MS, June 12.
	1963	March on Washington for Jobs & Freedom on August 28th
	1963	Assassination of President John Fitzgerald Kennedy
	1963	Lyndon Johnson assumed the Presidency on November 22nd

	Civil Rights Era
	Beginning of the Civil Rights Movement 1954
	1954 Brown v. Board of Education of Topeka
	1955, December Montgomery Bus Boycott
	1955, Lynching of Emmett Till
	1955, November 1st. Vietnam War start date (end of war April 1975 fall of Saigon)
	1958, January..31st NASA launch Explorer I ,
	Beginning of the Space Age
	John Fitzgerald. Kennedy 35th President 1961
	Assassination Medgar Evers, Jackson, MS June 12, 1963
	1963 August 28th, March on Washington for Jobs & Freedom
	Assassination of President John Fizgerald Kennedy (Dallas, TX, November 22, 1963)
	Lyndon Johnson assumed Presidency November 22,1963
	Civil Rights Act of 1964
	1965 Voting Rights Act -factors leading to the end of Jim (Factors leading to the end of Jim Crow Laws)
1966, August, Lorenzo Pitts, Jr. drafted into U.S. Navy	Assassination of Malcolm X: New York, NY February 21, 19651966
	Assassination of Martin Luther King, age 39, April 4, 1968
	1968, Civil Rights Act of 1968
	Assassination Robert F. Kennedy June 6, 1968, Los Angeles
	1970, Housing Urban Development ACT (HUD Act of 1970
	(Provides interest loans, grants, planning assistance, etc.)
	Watergate Scandal - President Richard Nixon Resigns August 9, 1974
	Gerald Ford assumed the Presidency August 9, 1974
	1977– 1981, 39th President James Earl Carter
	1981 -1989, 40th President Ronald Reagan to 1989
	1989 -1993, 41st President George H Bush to 1993
	1993 - 2001, 42nd President William (Bill) Clinton
1993 Multi-Family Property Disposition Program	1993 April 30th , Internet World-Wide Web available to public
Lorenzo Pitts Incorporated (LDP) Limited Denial Participation 1994, 1996	
HUD Owned Properties in Boston (LPI, Inc. 5 of 14)	2001 – 2009, 43rd President George Walker Bush
2005 Death of Rosalee Ridgell Pitts (November 14, 1931- February 13, 2005)	2008 Global financial crisis begins as stock market crashes.
	2009 - 2017, Barak Obama becomes 44th President (First African-American to hold office)

Lorenzo Pitts, Sr.death (Thymus Carcinoma) August 13, 1924 - Sept.3, 2009	
2009 Sr. Pitts' Estate - Suffolk County Probate Court October	
2011 – 2015 Suffolk Land Court – Pitts' Estate	2013- US Supreme Court Decision Shelby County v. Holder
2015 Mass. Appellate Court Filing– Pitts' Estate 2015	
Aug. 19, 2016, Appeals Court corrects Land County Desision	
	Reference: Voting Rights Act
	2017 – 2021, Donald Trump becomes 45th president
2017 Lorenzo Pitts, Jr. and Robert Pitts take possession of Esperanza Trust and Fort Hill Trust properties.	
	(HUD Boston Field Ofc reduced to Satellite of New York Ofc)
2018 (June 26) Jamaica Plain Neighborhood Development Corp. (JPNDC) Took possession of Pitts' Estate Properties,	
201 Units, 21 Bldgs. (Non-trust). Received $27.5 million from the City of Boston and Mass Housing to purchase and renovate the units	

APPENDIX G
TRIBUTES AND AWARDS

Awards – Plaques (Subcollection)

IN
CITY COUNCIL

BOSTON CITY COUNCILLORS CHARLES C. YANCEY & CHUCK TURNER

LORENZO PITTS, SR.

WHEREAS: Lorenzo Pitts, Sr. was born on August 13, 1924 to the late Napoleon Lee Pitts, Sr. and Minnie Lee Pitts in Hillsboro, Texas; And

WHEREAS: Mr. Pitts served in the United States Navy during the Second World War; And

WHEREAS: Mr. Pitts later migrated to the City of Boston, where he established a painting-paper hanging and small construction business; And

WHEREAS: Mr. Pitts' business expanded to function as a successful real estate agent and real estate property manager in the City of Boston for over 30 years; And

WHEREAS: Mr. Pitts was called home to the Lord on September 3, 2009, after battling a short illness; And

WHEREAS: Lorenzo Pitts, Sr. leaves to cherish his memory six sisters and brothers, 37 grandchildren and 32 great grandchildren; Be It Therefore

RESOLVED: That the Boston City Council, in meeting assembled; extends its deepest sympathy to the family of Lorenzo Pitts, Sr., in the passing of your loved one; And Be It Further

RESOLVED: That the Boston City Council, in meeting assembled, acknowledges the passing of Lorenzo Pitts, Sr., in whose memory all members stood in tribute and reverence as the Boston City Council adjourned its meeting of September 16, 2009.

By: _____
President of the City Council

Attest: _____
Clerk of the City of Boston

Offered by: _____

Date: September 16th, 2009

Massachusetts Housing Aqard of Achivement Award

From Sharecropper to Multimillionaire

NAACP Life Membership

Massachusetts Housing Finance Agency Award of Achievement

From Sharecropper to Multimillionaire

> **THE GROVE HALL BOARD OF TRADE**
> is proud to present this
> *LONGEVITY AWARD*
> to
> **LORENZO PITTS**
> in recognition and appreciation
> of your distinguished service
> and outstanding performance
> in the
> Greater Roxbury community.
>
> Presented This 6th Day of November, 1993
> Robert Hector, President

Grover Hall Board of Trade Distinguished Service

The National Black MBA Community Business Achievement

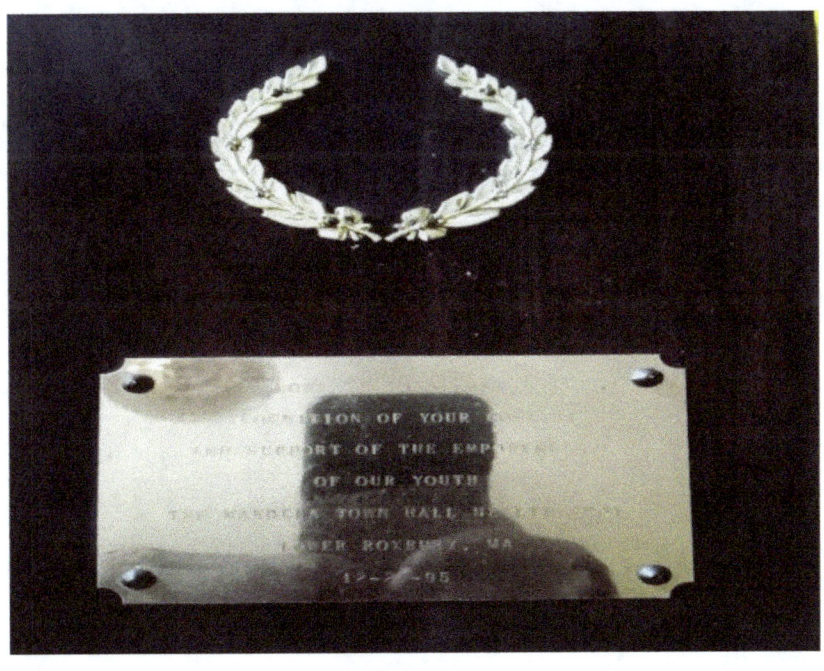

Mandela Town Hall Health SPOT Commitment and Support

National Center for Housing Management HUD Continuing Education

APPENDIX H
MOND/PITTS CORRESPONDENCE

LORENZO PITTS, INC.

UNANIMOUS CONSENT OF STOCKHOLDER

The undersigned, under authority granted by order of the Suffolk County Probate Court and in their capacity as Temporary Co-Executors of the Estate of Lorenzo Pitts, the sole Stockholder of Lorenzo Pitts, Inc. (the "Corporation"), and in accordance with the provisions of Section 7.04 of Chapter 156D of the General Laws of Massachusetts, hereby consent in writing on behalf of the Estate of Lorenzo Pitts to the following:

VOTED: That the number of Directors of the Corporation, unless changed by a vote of the Stockholders, be set at three (3); and

VOTED: That Lorenzo Pitts, Jr., Willetta Pitts and Terry K. Mond are hereby appointed as Directors of the Corporation, to serve until successors are duly elected and qualified.

Executed this 5th day of January, 2011.

ESTATE OF LORENZO PITTS

By: _____
Willetta Pitts, Temporary
Co-Executor

By: _____
Terry K. Mond, Temporary
Co-Executor

By: _____
Lorenzo Pitts, Jr., Temporary
Co-Executor

S. CLAUDIA LANG PITTS

GORDON, MOND & OTT, PC
ATTORNEYS AT LAW

Barry J. Gordon | Terry K. Mond | Roderick O. Ott | Cynthia B. Hartman | Matthew W. Gendreau

February 22, 2011

VIA FEDERAL EXPRESS, EMAIL
AND REGULAR MAIL
Dr. Lorenzo Pitts, Jr.
7915 Kiverton Place
Sandy Springs, GA 30350

Dear Dr. Pitts:

I am writing this letter on behalf of myself and Willetta Pitts-Givens, Temporary Co-Executors of the Estate of Lorenzo Pitts. It is with extreme dismay that I recently learned of your most recent extended absence, covering the two-week period from about February 14 through February 28, from the offices of Lorenzo Pitts, Inc. This comes on the heels of another absence running from before Christmas to the second week of January. This is simply unacceptable. As an employee of Lorenzo Pitts, Inc., you have the same responsibilities to keep regular hours as every other employee. On May 20, 2010, I wrote you an email where I made clear that you could not take long absences from the job and expect to be paid as a full-time employee. I can supply you a copy of that email at your request.

It has also become clear to me that you are no longer making any significant contribution to the operations of Lorenzo Pitts, Inc. Willetta Pitts has indicated that she does not know how you spend your time at the office, but that as far as she knows, you are not involved in any of the essential functions of the business, and on those occasions when you have been asked to do something, you routinely refuse. Other employees report that your interaction with them is largely limited to either criticizing them or expressing your opinion that the business was going to fail and that they would soon be out of a job because the business was going to shut down. You have had ample time to define a role that would contribute to the success of the business, but for reasons that are known only to you, you have chosen not to do so. That being the case, it is time that changes are made.

You indicated to Willetta in December and again more recently that, if management of the Pitts properties was not going to be transferred to Winn (as you have been advocating for some time), then you would want to go to, as you described it, "Plan B", where you would return to Atlanta and perhaps work remotely as a part-time

1 Batterymarch Park, Suite 312, Quincy, MA 02169   P: 617.786.0800   F: 617.786.9772   www.gmo-law.com

Dr. Lorenzo Pitts, Jr.
February 22, 2011
Page 2

employee. We have waited patiently for your proposal. If you intend to make a proposal along those lines, you need to do so immediately (meaning within the next seven days). Any such proposal should set out in detail exactly what responsibilities you propose to carry out remotely from Atlanta, and the number of hours per month you believe would be required to carry them out. The Co-Executors will seriously consider any proposal you may present, as long as the work you propose to do is specific and verifiable, and the proposed compensation is commensurate with the work.

If you are going to present a proposal, it must be before me no later than next Tuesday, March 1, 2011. Similarly, any negotiations that might ensue must be concluded no later than March 15, 2011. In the event of a failure for you to meet either of these deadlines, steps will be taken immediately thereafter to terminate your employment with Lorenzo Pitts, Inc. Given the current financial situation of the company, it simply cannot afford to pay any employee who doesn't make a significant contribution.

Just for clarification, the above does not affect your position as a Temporary Co-Executor of the Estate of Lorenzo Pitts. I expect you will continue in that capacity and participate in all decision making unless you indicate that you also wish to resign that position.

Very truly yours,

Terry K. Mond
Temporary Co-Executor of the
Estate of Lorenzo Pitts

cc: Willetta Pitts

S. CLAUDIA LANG PITTS

March 15, 2011

Dr. Lorenzo Pitts, Secretary
Lorenzo Pitts, Inc.
270 Roxbury Street
Roxbury, MA 02119

Dear Dr. Pitts:

The undersigned represent the Estate of Lorenzo Pitts, the sole stockholder of Lorenzo Pitts, Inc., a Massachusetts corporation ("the Corporation."), and are thus entitled to vote at a special meeting of stockholders to elect directors.

We hereby make application that you call a special meeting of stockholders in lieu of the annual meeting of stockholders of the Corporation. We demand that you call this meeting at 2:00 P.M., at the offices of the Corporation, 270 Roxbury Street, Roxbury, Massachusetts on the 21st day of March, 2011, for the following purpose:

To consider and act on a proposal to elect Lorenzo Pitts, Jr., Willetta Pitts and Terry K. Mond, directors of Lorenzo Pitts, Inc., to serve until successors are duly elected and qualified.

No other business shall be considered or acted upon at the meeting or any adjournment or adjournments thereof.

Very truly yours,

ESTATE OF LORENZO PITTS

By: _____
Willetta Pitts, Temporary Co-Executor

By: _____
Terry K. Mønd, Temporary Co-Executor

From Sharecropper to Multimillionaire

March 15, 2011

Dr. Lorenzo Pitts
270 Roxbury Street
Roxbury, MA 02119

691 River Street #6
Hyde Park, MA 02136

7915 Kiverton Place
Sandy Springs, GA 30350

Terry K. Mond, Esquire
One Batterymarch Park, #312
Quincy, MA 02169

Ms. Willetta Pitts
4 Stonehill Terrace
Hyde Park, MA 02126

Dear Sirs and Madam:

Please be advised that, pursuant to M.G.L.A. Chapter 156D, Section 8.22(b), a special meeting of the Board of Directors of Lorenzo Pitts, Inc. (the "Corporation") shall be held on Monday, March 21, 2011 at 2:00 P.M. or immediately following a special meeting of the Stockholders of the Corporation, at the offices of the Corporation at 270 Roxbury Street, Roxbury, Massachusetts. The purposes of the meeting are as follows:

1. To elect Willetta Pitts President of the Corporation, to serve until a successor is duly elected and qualified.

2. To elect Willetta Pitts Treasurer of the Corporation, to serve until a successor is duly elected and qualified..

3. To elect Terry K. Mond Secretary of the Corporation, to serve until a successor is duly elected and qualified.

4. To terminate the employment of Lorenzo Pitts, Jr., effective immediately.

No other business shall be considered or acted upon at the meeting or any adjournment or adjournments thereof.

Very truly yours,

Willetta Pitts, Director

Terry K. Mond, Director

APPENDIX I
MEDIA ARTICLES

From Sharecropper to Multimillionaire

Boston Bulletin
citywide news • street by street

VOLUME 12, NUMBER 50   JULY 26, 2018   FREE

JPNDC preserves housing for 200 families
Takes ownership of 21 buildings

One of the buildings acquired by JPNDC is the 1881 Louis Prang Chromolithography plant on Roxbury and Gardner streets.
PHOTO BY: RICHARD HEATH

Richard Heath
Staff Reporter

On June 26, the Jamaica Plain Neighborhood Development Corporation (JPNDC) took ownership of 21 multifamily buildings totaling 201 units for $22 million.

"This is by far the largest single project we've ever been involved with," said Richard Thal, executive director of the JPNDC.

The properties are in four parcels on three streets near Grove Hall off Blue Hill Avenue, in the Mt Pleasant neighborhood above Dudley Square, and on Roxbury Street behind Roxbury Community College.

Owned by the Lorenzo Pitts Company since 1992, the Pitts family – when Lorenzo died in 2009 at the age of 93 – sought legal advice regarding the properties' title – an issue that was resolved in 2015.

The Pitts estate put out an RFP (request for proposals) for the sale of the properties in 2017.

JPNDC Housing
Continued on page 15

Solar canopies coming to Roslindale Station

Roslindale's Commuter Rail Station could soon be seeing solar canopies over parking spaces next year.
COURTESY PHOTO

Jeff Sullivan
Staff Reporter

Earlier this year, the MBTA announced it would be installing solar panels canopies at 34 Commuter Rail Stations across its network.

In Boston, that means Wonderland and Roslindale Stations are getting the new solar canopies, that will cover selected spaces in the stations' parking lots. The MBTA has partnered with MAP Energy Funding Solutions and Omni Navitas Solar Energy Development to install the canopies across the MBTA's rail network.

According to Massachusetts Department of Transportation (MassDOT) Spokesperson Lisa Battiston, the project is slated to hit Roslindale hopefully in the fall of 2018.

According to Chief of MBTA Real Estate Janelle Chan, Roslindale and Wonderland are not prioritized in the scheduling because the MBTA wanted to finalize agreements and construction start dates with municipalities that have their own municipal energy distribution systems.

"Solar panel work, which includes the installation of solar panel canopies, is currently in the construction phase at Nantasket Junction, West Hingham, and Norwood Central Stations," said Battiston. "Completion of solar panel canopies at these stations is anticipated by fall 2018."

Battison also said that, though Roslindale is slated for solar panels, the MBTA still has to complete its approval process for the site.

Solar Canopy
Continued on page 14

Slow Streets in Roslindale coming together

About 40 residents came out to see what the city had in store for the installation of traffic calming measures in Mount Hope/Mount Canterbury.
PHOTO BY JEFF SULLIVAN

Jeff Sullivan
Staff Reporter

Last week, City of Boston Active Transportation Director Stefanie Seskin came to the Home for Little Wanderers in Roslindale to show the community the city's plan to make the streets in the neighborhoods around American Legion Highway a bit safer.

The neighborhood was one of five that received a grant for implementing Slow Streets earlier this year, and Seskin came to show some preliminary ideas the city has to ease traffic concerns. Ba-

Slow Streets
Continued on page 13

Cleary Square development leads HPNA to Sprague Street

Matt MacDonald
Staff Reporter

The Hyde Park Neighborhood Association (HPNA) met on Thursday, July 5 in the community room of the Area E-18 Police Station located at 1249 Hyde Park Ave.

Approximately 20 people attended the monthly meeting, the main topic of which was the introduction of a proposed residential/commercial development in the Cleary Square area.

Attorney John Pulgini – representing developer Milan Patel, who was present but largely silent, aside from letting the group know that he lives on the North Shore and that he has other properties in Somerville and Boston – went before the HPNA to present early stage

Attorney John Pulgini takes a question from a member of the Hyde Park Neighborhood Association at 11 Dana Ave. developer Milan Patel currently at that address and to replace it with a 24-unit building.
Photo By Matt MacDonald

information and diagrams for a project proposed for 11 Dana Ave.

The lot – located in the section of Dana Avenue between Hyde Park Avenue and the parking lot of the Hyde Park commuter rail station – currently holds a three-family house.

HPNA
Continued on page 12

161

July 26, 2018   The Bulletin

JPNDC Housing continued from page 1

"The Pitts family had issues with taxes and subsidies," Thal said. "And they hired Peabody Properties last year to help untangle those problems."

Peabody Properties has long been the property manager for JPNDC's residential holdings.

"One thing the Pitts family told us was these properties are an important part of Lorenzo Pitts' legacy," Thal said."JPNDC has had, over the past 10 years, a lot of experience with financing... We feel like we can work on increasingly complex projects with multiple financing sources, the subsidy contracts and historic tax credits. We feel we have the capacity to do sophisticated projects."

One of the problems with the properties was the project-based subsidies, most had expired years ago, with the Pitts Company continuing since then with one year renewals.

"This keeps them going but you want long term assurances for the tenants," said Thal.

JPNDC is the third owner of these 21 buildings. In 1966 MassHousing Finance Agency (MassHousing) was created by the state legislature to provide loans to proven developers who could demonstrate their ability to rehabilitate and manage older rental housing, much of which was abandoned.

JPNDC is in the process now of meeting with the residents and Peabody Properties managers are reviewing income re-certification and leases.

A relocation specialist has also been meeting with residents because some may have to move out for a few weeks during rehabilitation of their apartments.

"One of the things we talked about at the annual meeting this year," Thal said, "was how

"We're really excited that 155 units have a 20-year, project-based subsidies to keep them affordable with Section 8 vouchers. We're certain we can get that in perpetuity," he added.

The City of Boston provided acquisition funding for the at-risk units through the Acquisition Opportunity Program (AOP) launched in May 2016. Mayor Walsh allocated $7.5 million in Inclusionary Development funds to support the acquisition of occupied rental housing. Through AOP, 137 units in the Pitts housing will be preserved for a minimum of 50 years, with 14 reserved for formerly homeless individuals and families.

In announcing the program the Mayor was specific about its purpose. "This program ensured that Boston residents will not be priced out of their homes and neighborhoods", he said.

The remaining units will be underwritten with MassHousing funds and tax

Page 15

JPNDC benefits other neighborhoods. We said that 80 percent of the people who come to our small business programs, our financial literacy or other programs come from as far away as East Boston. Many used to live in JP. Some heard about the good word about us. We're clearly providing services to a wider community."

MassHousing recognizes that the investment it first made nearly 50 years ago is being sustained.

"JPNDC is a high-capacity mission-driven organization," MassHousing's Paul McMorrow said. "We thank the JPNDC and the Pitts estate for their ongoing commitment to the residents of these properties for decades to come."

credit funding.

MassHousing issued a statement on the matter:

"The roughly $45.7 million of MassHousing funds will finance the full acquisition, rehabilitation and preservation of all 201 of the Pitts portfolio as affordable housing."

The other major problem was the condition of some of the buildings: most which were built between 1911 and 1913, with two built about 1880.

The total rehabilitation of all 21 buildings will total $30 million phased over 20 months beginning in the fall of 2018.

Thal said he expects the rehabilitation to be completed in mid-2020 and will include roof replacement, new windows, electrical and heating upgrades and selected new kitchens and baths. The Architectural Team will do design and construction plans. One of the buildings located at 74-76 Intervale St. and built in 1968, was issued a building permit on June 4 for $244,000 in renovations.

From Sharecropper to Multimillionaire

JPNDC rehabilitates Lorenzo Pitts units

Boston Mayor Kim Janey cuts the ribbon on newly-renovated affordable units on
PHOTO: AVERY BLEICHFELD

By AVERY BLEICHFELD

More than 200 units of income-restricted housing across Roxbury and parts of Dorchester will be kept affordable, according to the Jamaica Plain Neighborhood Development Corporation (JPNDC).

The units, comprising a portfolio of 21 buildings in Fort Hill, Nubian Square and Grove Hall, were owned by Lorenzo Pitts until his death in 2009. Pitts, a Roxbury-based housing owner and developer, left a mandate that the units be kept affordable.

But in 2016, about 150 of those units were at risk of being converted to market-rate housing, said Teronda Ellis, CEO of JPNDC, at a ribbon-cutting event Tuesday. Her organization, which works to develop affordable housing across the city, felt that it was important to keep the properties affordable.

"It wasn't a question of whether, but of how we do that with our partners," Ellis said.

What followed was a five-year process complicated by the COVID-19 pandemic on top of the challenges inherent to renovating units with residents living in them.

During the renovations, residents had to be temporarily moved out while construction teams could move in — typically for about three weeks, according to JPNDC.

But, despite the difficulties and the additional challenges the pandemic brought, the important piece of the work was making sure residents had safe and affordable housing, said Chrystal Kornegay, the executive director of MassHousing, a state-level agency that helps provide financing for affordable housing and was involved in the JPNDC Pitts Apartments project.

> "We're building homes for people; we're keeping people's homes nice, because the one thing that we may have known, but that the whole globe knows now, is how fundamental home is in every aspect of your life."
> – Chrystal Kornegay

"At the end of the day, we understand that it's about the people," Kornegay said. "We're not just doing pretty buildings or rehabs or complicated structures. We're building homes for people; we're keeping people's homes nice, because the one thing that we may have known, but how fundamental home is in every aspect of your life."

According to a release from the City of Boston, of the 201 units, 14 are restricted to households earning up to 30% of the area median income (AMI), 161 are restricted to tenants at or below 60% AMI and 26 are restricted to at or below 80% of the AMI. 165 of the units are supported by Section 8 vouchers or other subsidies.

Phaedra Bruton-Paige, a local activist and resident of one of the buildings for more than 25 years, was grateful for the renovations. She said that keeping the community together allows for more positive change.

"To push us out of here does not make it better, it does not give us knowledge, it just makes us feel that we're just thrown away," Bruton-Paige said. "We don't want anyone to feel like they're thrown away, because Boston is the place to be."

Acting Mayor Kim Janey attended the ribbon-cutting. She described a personal history with affordable housing and being priced out of gentrifying neighborhoods in Boston. Citing increasing housing prices in the city, she said the JPNDC Pitts portfolio was an important step in making sure residents can stay in their neighborhoods.

"I think this is an important model for us to replicate as we do all we can to create the housing we need in the city of Boston," Janey said. "We know there was a housing crisis long before COVID-19 and that COVID has made this worse."

The same sentiment was expressed by Sheila Dillon, chief of Housing and director of Neighborhood Development for the City of Boston.

"We want to build, we want to build back better, we want to continue building affordable housing, but if we don't hold onto what we have, families will be harmed and we won't have net new affordable homes," Dillon said.

At the event, both Dillon and Janey referred to actions the acting mayor has taken to support housing since taking office in March. For instance, Janey worked with the City Council to set aside $20 million in the 2022 budget for the Acquisition Opportunity Program, which the city uses to help investors buy occupied multi-family properties while creating protections for current tenants.

They said Janey has also called for federal COVID-19 relief money from the American Rescue Plan (ARP) to be used for affordable housing. According to the city's 2022 budget, $30 million is set aside from the ARP to be used for emergency rental assistance relief and housing.

Despite the challenges of the process with the JPNDC Pitts apartments, Ellis said the completion of the project is an important step in supporting the residents in the 201 units and their communities.

"We have 201 safe, good-looking units and amazing families who can be sure that what's going on behind the walls and at the roof level and at the windows ... that they're safe," Ellis said. "And now, the work starts — now the work starts on rebuilding with the JPNDC; conversations will start on what's next."

Janey and JPNDC cut ribbon on affordable housing units

Acting Mayor Kim Janey shown with members of the JPNDC, MassHousing and residents of the Pitts Portfolio building cutting the ribbon on the new apartments.

By Gazette Staff

Last Tuesday, Mayor Kim Janey joined the Jamaica Plain Neighborhood Development Corporation (JPNDC), MassHousing and the residents of multiple affordable housing sites, collectively called the Pitts Portfolio, to celebrate the acquisition, preservation and renovation of 201 units in Roxbury and Dorchester.

JPNDC utilized $1.5 million in City of Boston Acquisition Opportunity Program (AOP) funding and $26 million in permanent MassHousing financing to purchase and renovate the units. This funding allowed for extensive capital improvements across the 201 unit portfolio, as well as finance the long-term affordability of the properties. As part of the work, 11 units were made accessible to people with disabilities and 14 units have been set aside to house formerly homeless individuals and families.

"This is a great example of how community partners can work together to ensure Boston residents

When JPNDC acquired the Pitts Portfolio in 2018, only 64 of the 201 units had long-term affordability restrictions, and without a long-term preservation transaction, the remainder were at risk of being converted to market-rate housing. The City's $1.5M in AOP funding helped to ensure that all 201 units will have long-term affordability.

"Welcome home to all the residents of the Lorenzo Pitts properties who now have renovated, modern homes where they can live affordably and prosper well into the future," said MassHousing Executive Director Chrystal Kornegay. "MassHousing commends the Jamaica Plain Neighborhood Development Corporation and the estate of Lorenzo Pitts – as well as the city, state and private partners involved in this project - for their commitment to preserving this important affordable housing portfolio in Dorchester and Roxbury."

Overall, there are 38 one-bedroom apartments, 87 two-bedroom apartments, 53 three-bedroom apartments, 18 four-bedroom placement at selected buildings, accessibility upgrades, kitchen and bathroom upgrades, and mechanical, electrical and plumbing system upgrades.

Of the 201 units in the Pitts portfolio, 14 units are restricted to households earning 30 percent of Area Median Income (AMI) or less, 161 units are restricted at or below 60 percent of the Area Median Income (AMI) and 26 units are restricted at or below 80 percent of

have a place to call home," said Janey at the ribbon cutting last week" The ability of the City to keep these units affordable into the future is a huge win for Boston. I look forward to continuing to work with our nonprofit organizations, MassHousing and other partners to protect and preserve Boston's affordable housing options."

The housing is located in 21 buildings in Fort Hill, Nubian Square and Grove Hall, purchased from the estate of Lorenzo Pitts. Mr. Pitts was a successful, Roxbury-based owner and housing developer. Most of the units were affordable to low-income families.

APPENDIX J
SUGGESTED READING LIST AND VIDEOS

Suggested Reading List

Black AF History. The Un-Whitewashed Story of America. Author Michael Harriot. Copyright 2023. HarperCollins Publishers, New York, NY

Black Codes In Georgia. Compiled By Dan Moore, Sr. ad Michele Mitchell. Copyright 2006. Published by The APEX Museum

Deep Roots. How Slavery Still Shapes Southern Politics. By Avidit Acharya, Matthew Blackwell, and Maya Sen. Copyright 2018. Published by Princeton University Press.

From Slavery to Freedom. By John Hope Franklin and Alfred A. Moss, Jr. Published September 22, 1947. Seventh Edition 1994 by McGraw-Hill, Inc.

Generational Wealth. Author Nicholas Charles and Antoneta Proctor. Published July 6, 2022. Writing Matters Publishing.

James Oglethorpe, Father of Georgia, A Founders Journey From, Slave Trader to Abolitionist. Author Michael L. Thurmond. Copyright 2024 by Michael L. Thurmond. The University of Georgia Press, Athens

Lynching in America, Confronting the Legacy of Racial Terror. By Equal Justice Initiative. Copyright 2017 Montgomery, Alabama 36104.
Preserving General Wealth. Author Douglas Eze, A,C. Published August 1, 2024. Publisher Largo Financial Service Inc.
Reconstruction in America, Racial Violence after the Civil War, 1865-1876. By Equal Justice Initiative. Copyright 2020. Montgomery, Alabama 36104.
Reconstruction in Texas. By Charles William Ramsdell, Ph.D. Columbia University, New York. Copyright, 1910.
Segregation in America. Copyright 2018 Montgomery, Alabama 36104.
Slavery By Another Name, The Re-Enslavement of Black Americans from the Civil War to World War II. Author, Douglas A. Blackmon. Copyright 2008 By Douglas A. Blackmon. Published in the USA by Anchor Books, a division of Random House, Inc. New York..2008.
Slavery in America, The Montgomery Slave Trade. By Equal Justice Initiative. Copyright 2018 Montgomery, Alabama 36104.
The First Waco Horror, The Lynching of Jesse Washington and The Rise of the NAACP. Author Patricia Bernstein. Copyright 2005. Third printing 2008 Library of Congress Cataloging-in-Publication
The Hands of Persons Unknown, The Lynching of Black America. Author Philip Dray. Copyright 2002. Published by Random House, Inc.
The Negro Law of the South Carolina. Collected and Digested by John Belton O'Neall. Printed By John G. Bowman, 1848
Through The Codes Darkly, Slave Law and Civil Law in Louisiana. By Vernon Valentine Palmer. Copyright 2012. The Lawbook Exchange, Ltd., Clark, New Jersey

Suggested Videos: (YouTube)

40 Acres and a Mule. CBS News Report. Sparta, Georgia
Debt Slavery (Sharecropping). Aboriginal Americans
Did Slavery Continue after the Civil War? Heimler's History
How Sharecroppers Became Debt Slaves. Documentary Clips Stack Stories – Sharecropping
Lest We Forget: The Lost Story of Southern Sharecroppers. Xion Lester
Mary and Early William on Life as a Sharecropper. Voices of / Ben L Hooks institute
Sharecropping. Marginal Revolution University.
Sharecropping. Mike Vance Writer
Sharecropping. NBC News Learn. Sharecropping in the Post-Civil War South.
Sharecropping in the American South. Daily Dose Documentary
Sharecroppers of the Great Depression. Donnie Laws.
Sharecropping: The Cycles of Poverty and Mistreatment. Jamie Puckett
Slavery by Another Name: Sharecropping #History. Aaron: The Rebel Historian – Shorts
What is Sharecropping? University of Memphis Studies Explained

APPENDIX K
PHOTO ARCHIVES

Esperanza Trust 42 Units

Lorenzo Pitts, Sr. PORTFOLIO NON-TRUST PROPERTIES (Subcollection)

Lorenzo Sr. and Lorenzo Jr. Inspection Day

691 River Street, Hyde Park - Private

Lorenzo Pitts, Inc. Office, 270 Roxbury Steet

Artist Charles Scogins

NOTES

Prologue

1. Encyclopedia of Arkansas. *Separate Coach Law of 1891*
2. https://www.goodreads.com/quotes/413318-we-see-a-hearse-we-think-sorrow-we-see-a

Chapter 1

1. https://www.nbcdfw.com/news/call-for-change/sherman-texas-group-pushes-for-a-historical-marker-to-remember-1930-race-riot/2734699/
2. https://www.icp.org/browse/archive/objects/body-of-george-hughes-hanging-from-a-tree-sherman-texas
3. https://www.washingtonpost.com/history/2021/06/03/sherman-riot-texas-lynching-marker/

Chapter 2

1. National Archives photo – new recruits.
2. https://en.wikipedia.org.wiki.USSNitro:(AE-2)
3. 1 https://en.wikipedia.org/wiki/USS_Francis_M._Robinson

Chapter 6

1. https://en.m.wikipedia.org. "List of Colleges and Universities in Metropolitan Boston." "Sports in Boston." "History of Boston."
2. Ibid
3. www.khanacademy.org Khan Academy, The GI Bill. Article written by Dr. Kimberly Kutz Elliott
4. https://www.history.com/articles/black-soldiers-world-war-ii-discrimination
5. Selve 2021 McNulty, Moving Past Dysfunctional Families 09/07/2022
6. Reed 2021 McNulty, Moving Past Dysfunctional Families 09/07/2022

www.ingramcontent.com/pod-product-compliance
Lightning Source LLC
Chambersburg PA
CBHW050256010526
44107CB00033B/1397/J